Correlli Barnett was co-scriptwriter and historical consultant to the landmark BBC television series *The Great War*, for which he won (with John Terraine) the 1964 Screenwriters' Guild Award for Best Documentary Script. Born in 1927, he was educated at Trinity School, Croydon and read Modern History at Exeter College, Oxford. He is a Fellow of Churchill College, Cambridge, where he was Keeper of the Churchill Archives Centre between 1977 and 1995. Correlli Barnett is National President of the Western Front Association. In 1991 he was awarded the Chesney Gold Medal of the Royal United Services Institute for Defence Studies, and in 1993 an honorary Doctorate of Science by Cranfield University. In 1997 he was appointed CBE for his services to military history.

His many other books include *The Desert Generals* (1960), *The Swordbearers* (1963), *Britain and Her Army* (1970), *Engage the Enemy More Closely: The Royal Navy in the Second World War* (1991, winner of the *Yorkshire Post* Book of the Year Award) and the 'Pride and Fall' sequence: *The Collapse of British Power* (1972), *The Audit of War* (1986), *The Lost Victory* (1995) and *The Verdict of Peace* (2001).

the
great war

CORRELLI BARNETT

This edition published in 2003 to accompany the re-transmission on BBC2 of the television series *The Great War*, first broadcast in 1964. Text first published in hardback by Park Lane Press, 1979.

ISBN 0 563 48887 5

Published by BBC Worldwide Limited
Woodlands, 80 Wood Lane, London W12 0TT

Printed and bound in Great Britain by Butler & Tanner Ltd, Frome
Origination by Radstock Reproductions Ltd, Midsomer Norton

Front cover: British and French soldiers on the Western Front in 1916.
Back cover: Armistice Day celebrations in London, 11 November 1918.

Contents

For Ruth, who, as wife, mother, grandmother and all-purpose support group, still does so much.

Foreword

THE MEMORY OF THE GREAT WAR OF 1914–18 haunts us still, even after the passing of more than eighty years and a second world conflict that cost more than twice as many lives. Today, in novels and television dramas, the soldiers are still bidding farewell to their families in villages and back streets, shouldering their packs, and going off to the front; Edwardian society is still living out its last gracious hours before expiring under the impact of total war.

Historians continue to debate the war's causes, conduct and consequences. A few glibly argue that Britain could, and should, have avoided the human and economic costs of the war by staying neutral, and instead lived with the inevitable result – a Europe dominated by a victorious imperial Germany; militaristic, expansionist and autocratic. Other historians continue to regurgitate the cliché that the war amounted to no more than futile mass slaughter, even though it ended in victory for the democracies, and even though it was the follies of politicians *after* the war that by the 1930s had rendered futile the soldiers' victory.

In Britain and America especially, there abides among some historians an emotional revulsion against the terrible fact that a war between great military and industrial powers inevitably means a long struggle of attrition, costly in human life. They look for scapegoats. And where better than among the high command? This is why they choose to harp on the stalemated trench warfare battles of the Somme and Passchendaele, rather than celebrate the victorious Allied offensives of 1918, which, under the same commanders, forced Germany to sue for an armistice. Such English-speaking historians have been so influenced by the lamentations of an unrepresentative handful of middle-class soldier-poets and novelists that they have forgotten that the British army was the only army on either side of the Western Front never to suffer a serious crisis of morale.

In contrast, there is a school of younger historians whose researches bear out this book's contention that to create and equip from scratch a mass British citizen army and within four years turn it into the most formidable fighting machine on the Western Front was an amazing achievement. The popular myth that the generals and staffs were blockheads, remote from the front line realities and unable or unwilling to profit from experience, is being steadily refuted by investigation into the British army's 'learning curve' of tactical study, experiment and innovative change.

The war has now become part of the National Curriculum in British schools. The battlefields and war cemeteries of France and Belgium are thronged with visiting schoolchildren. We who in

1964 made *The Great War* television series, which first brought the history of the conflict to family audiences around the world, could never have imagined that in the next century there would continue to be so keen a general interest in the war.

What accounts for this abiding fascination? It is the hankering of our own confused and troubled age for the seeming certainties of a time when everyone knew their place and duty. It is a deep nostalgia for the lost innocence and faith of the generation that went to war in 1914 believing in a cause, living by such virtues and comradeship, discipline and courage, and ready to die, if need be, for King and Country, Kaiser and Fatherland, or *La Patrie*. It is our sense of wonder at the cheerful stoicism that enabled the soldiers of the opposing armies to endure four long years of unremitting hardship and danger.

Yet the Great War holds other, deeper, meanings for us. It marked the birth of our own age, abruptly hastening the march of equality and mass participation, liberating women from political and domestic thraldom, thrusting forward technological change, creating independent nations in place of empires, and republics in place of monarchies. It marked the origins of the present turbulence in the Middle East. It created in Soviet Russia the first Communist state, and ushered the United States of America to the centre of the world stage for the first time.

In the history of this tragic, titanic struggle lies the essential key to an understanding of the world we live in today.

Correlli Barnett
East Carleton, Norfolk, January 2003

Introduction

JOHN TERRAINE

MY ROLE AS PRINCIPAL SCRIPTWRITER and historical consultant to the 1964 BBC television series *The Great War* presented a unique professional challenge, demanding that the war's vast complexities be reduced to a comprehensible simplicity of narrative, and that the words be married to archive film and photographs with an incomparably powerful impact of their own. It must be remembered that the project was without precedent in documentary television for sheer scale and ambitiousness of vision. In 26 episodes of 40 minutes each it was to cover all the fronts (including the home fronts) in the most terrible conflict experienced by mankind up to that time. And the challenge to the scriptwriter was all the more daunting because of the ever faster pace with which the 26 episodes had to be produced in order to meet the transmission dates – and also because the senior producer himself, Tony Essex, was an impatient film-making genius who approached his task with deep historical convictions of his own. It was he who framed the broad strategy of the series in the form of one-page statements of the themes of each of the 26 programmes. My memory is that in the event we did not find it necessary to change more than about five of those themes – which is a tremendous tribute to Essex's penetration and understanding.

All these factors generated a high creative heat within the production team, whether film editors, scriptwriters, film and picture researchers, or interviewers of Great War veterans on camera. This creative heat forged a final product which proved an outstanding success with viewers and critics alike on its first transmission in 1964. Today *The Great War* series is recognized by historians of documentary film-making as a major innovative breakthrough, and by historians of the Great War itself as a unique visual and narrative record of the first global conflict of the industrial age.

I therefore warmly welcome the BBC's decision to screen the series again; and especially because nowadays there is a keener interest than ever among our young people in the Great War, and in the Western Front in particular.

It is perhaps understandable that, as a rule, young people first approach the subject through the profoundly moving personal testimony of the trench poets, novelists and memorialists – men such as Robert Graves, Siegfried Sassoon and Wilfred Owen. Nevertheless, this testimony can be a misleading guide simply because it *is* so personal, so intensely subjective. The trench literature has been very largely responsible for the abiding myth in British minds that the Great War, and particularly the Western

Front, amounted to no more than futile mass slaughter conducted by callous and incompetent military leaders.

I am inclined to believe that the British, more than others of the belligerent nations, have found it hard to pass beyond sheer emotional reaction to the terrible experiences of the men in uniform to a comprehension of the intractable grand-strategic dilemmas that shaped those experiences. To the British, long accustomed to small colonial conflicts, the scale of this war and the resulting losses were unprecedented and shocking. All too often in British accounts – especially in theatrical caricatures such as the musical *Oh What a Lovely War* or the television comedy series *Blackadder Goes Forth* – there is an overemphasis on the British role and British casualties, almost as if the war were just a contest between the German and British Empires, and no other allied army had to fight battles like the Somme or Third Ypres ('Passchendaele').

And so we sought in *The Great War* series to redress the balance by describing in film and script the large parts played by other countries – such as the terrible battles fought by the French in 1915 while Britain was still creating her mass citizen army, and the later French martyrdom at Verdun in 1916; such as the titanic struggles on the Eastern Front between Tsarist Russia and the alliance of the German and the Austro-Hungarian empires.

Although the war was, of course, primarily a conflict between European powers, it eventually encompassed virtually the whole world. There were two reasons for this. The first was that some of the European powers had large imperial possessions spread across the world which were immediately drawn in – the British dominions of Canada, Australia, New Zealand and South Africa,

Britain's Indian Empire and her colonies in Africa and Asia; French possessions in Africa and Indo-China; Germany's colonies and outposts in Africa, the Far East and the Pacific; the Turkish Empire spread from the Bosporus and the Dardanelles to Syria, Palestine and the Persian Gulf. And secondly it became a world war because it was fought on the oceans, which made it virtually inevitable that another great maritime nation would sooner or later be involved: the United States of America.

Most historians – even German ones – now agree that Germany was the starting point of the conflict, as it was of the Second World War, for only the German war plan involved an automatic invasion of another country (France), whether or not that country itself intended to go to war. Only the German plan demanded that, in order to prosecute this invasion, neutral territory (Luxembourg and Belgium) had to be instantly violated, thereby provoking Great Britain to join in the conflict.

No war in history has been so subject to myth-making, especially myth-making that stands in constant need of correction by reference to cold fact. For instance, as long as people believe that the Great War was the *most* murderous and the *most* destructive, they will not understand it. Yet the truth is that the cost in human life in the Second World War of 1939–45 was approximately four times that in the Great War of 1914–18. It is a common British myth that the reason why Britain's own losses in the Second World War were only a third of those in the Great War lies in superior generalship. The true reason is that in 1916, 1917 and 1918 a massed British Expeditionary Force was fighting the main body of the German army on the most important battleground of the War – the Western Front – a far more exacting military task than the British army has ever performed before or since. In the Second World War the comparable British mass deployment on the Western Front lasted less than a year, from the D-Day invasion of Normandy in June 1944 to the final defeat of Nazi Germany in May 1945. It is therefore no wonder that British casualties in the Second World War were much smaller than in the Great War.

We must never forget that in the Second World War it was the Red Army of the Soviet Union on the Eastern Front that in five terrible years of struggle played the major part in gutting the German army, at a cost of 11 million Russian dead.

And we must anyway remember that Britain's losses in the Great War were smaller in proportion to national population than those of the other belligerents: 1.9 per cent, as against France's 3.5 per cent and Germany's 2.9 per cent.

It is hard to believe that these high rates of loss on both sides are simply to be explained on the grounds that a whole generation of highly trained military leaders – French, German, Russian, Italian, British, even American – were mere callous bunglers. The true explanation surely lies elsewhere – in the very nature of a war that was so novel in its vast scale and in the complexity of its challenges as to be beyond even perfectly able political and military talent of the time. In particular, no military leader on either side succeeded in solving the conundrum presented by the then state of military technology – tremendous destructive firepower from artillery and machine gun, but very poor battlefield communications (there were no 'walkie-talkie' radios), thus isolating commanders from their frontline units at critical moments; and a crippling lack of mobility, with cavalry effectively obsolete but tanks and motor transport still at their most primitive and unreliable. All these factors are vividly illustrated by the astonishing archive film found for *The Great War* series.

Nonetheless, the British should surely take pride as a nation in the rapid evolution by which Britain's raw citizen army of 1916 became – under the same generals – the highly professional 'all-arms' force of 1918, which played the major role in the victorious allied offensives that finally brought Germany to sue for an armistice.

But this was not only a conflict between men in uniform. Total war meant total mobilization of the social and industrial resources of the belligerent societies. Here was perhaps the grandest of all the novelties of 1914–18. In *The Great War* series, the programmes on this vital topic were written by my principal colleague as scriptwriter, the historian Correlli Barnett, with whom I shared the 1964 Screenwriters' Guild Award for the Best Documentary Script. In these programmes we see in operation the vast new green-field factories built to mass-produce artillery, shells and their explosive fillings, machine guns, aircraft, tanks and motor vehicles. We see the busy assembly lines staffed entirely by women. We see women working in civilian jobs, whether in offices, on the land, or in transport, that in peacetime had been the preserve of men. In this way the war offered women a liberation from domestic confinement, and served to vindicate their claim for a parliamentary vote.

But total war also demanded the full mobilization of science and technology. *The Great War* series shows in graphic film images the dreadful effects of accelerated invention: poison gas; the flame-thrower; the sinking victims of the U-boat, so nearly Britain's vanquisher in 1917; aircraft in all their variety of design, supplying the new dimension of warfare by land and sea; and the wreckage left by the first experiments in the strategic aerial bombing of enemy cities.

The Great War series therefore stands as a comprehensive, compelling and never surpassed filmic history of the conflict.

It fell to my friend Correlli Barnett to write this book, which closely follows the original narrative structure of the television series and incorporates much of the original research material. Correlli Barnett gives crystal-clear accounts of all the political and strategic dilemmas, as well as of the social and industrial impacts of total war. He combines these accounts with hauntingly evocative descriptions of men in battle and vivid portraits of the civilian and military leaderships on both sides as they sought that elusive prize, victory.

I therefore commend this book to all those who wish to understand the Great War, and especially to our young people.

John Terraine, January 2003

ONE
The lamps are going out

WHEN THE ARCHDUKE FRANZ FERDINAND AND HIS WIFE SOPHIE set off in an open car on Sunday, 28 June 1914, to pay an official visit to Sarajevo, the capital of the Austrian province of Bosnia, Europe seemed to be enjoying more settled peace than for many years. The tensions that had brought the great powers to the verge of war in 1905 and again in 1911 seemed at last to have relaxed. In 1912 good sense and moderation had prevented wars in the Balkans from exploding into a general conflict. All over Europe that Sunday respectable families went to church in celebration of the established order – father at the head of the family, the monarch at the head of the nation, and God in His heaven. Then came the peaceful Sunday pleasures: an afternoon on the beach or river; meandering along the dusty lanes by bicycle; a stroll in a city park listening to the band; and for the aristocracy and gentry at the apex of the social pyramid, tea on the lawn in a cedar's shade.

Kaiser Wilhelm II of Germany spent the day aboard his yacht at the elegant Kiel Regatta; President Poincaré of France at the races at Longchamps, amid gentlemen frock-coated in the summer sunshine and huge-hatted ladies brilliant in Poiret gowns.

With the exception of the French Republic, this was a Europe of kings and emperors – and a sultan, of Turkey. In St Petersburg the pious Tsar Nicholas II ruled over a Russian Empire extending from the borders of Germany and Austria to China and the Pacific; a country of vast spaces and poor communications, of backward peasant agriculture and a belated industrial revolution. In Vienna the old Habsburg Emperor Franz Josef united in his own person the multi-language peoples of Austria-Hungary – the German-speakers of Austria itself, the Czechs of Bohemia, the Poles of Galicia, the Hungarians, the South Slavs of the newly acquired Balkan provinces of Bosnia and Herzegovina. From Berlin Kaiser Wilhelm II – neurotic and vain – ruled a German Empire only united since 1871, a brash, powerful, ambitious newcomer among nation states; indeed, the major unsettling influence in Europe. For since 1871 Germany's industries had grown in huge bounds: her steel production had risen by more than 500 per cent, and now stood at twice the British figure. She possessed the greatest chemical industry in the world. Not content with the largest and most efficient army in Europe, she had challenged British command of the sea by creating a formidable high-seas fleet in hardly more than ten years. All this lay in the hands of an unstable monarch and governing circles that were determined to push Germany's claim to be a world power. And in London George V, the King-Emperor, reigned over the British

Empire – the empire that Germany most envied and wished to overtake. This empire was made up of India, wide tracts of Africa, Malaya, scattered islands in the Pacific, the whole of Ireland, and the self-governing dominions of Australia, New Zealand, Canada and South Africa.

It was the high noon of the nation state, recognizing no authority superior to itself, no morality beyond its own self-interest. This claim to untrammelled sovereignty was embodied in armed forces kept up to the greatest strength and preparedness that could be contrived. The courts, cabinets and foreign offices busied themselves with the traditional European power game, seeking to win advantages and parry threats by means of intrigue or intimidation. It was also the high noon of nationalism – even the rootless masses living grey existences in the new industrial towns found emotional escape in a romantic patriotism. They were stirred by symbols such as the national flag, as are modern football supporters by club emblems and colours. They exulted in the power represented by their nation's armed forces – troops on parade and clanging bands; battleships in line-ahead. 'Future war' fantasies encouraged their readers to think of war as an exciting adventure; a test of manliness. Even poets and artists could glamorize violence and war as means to cleanse the human spirit of the corruption of peace. Influential thinkers garbled the biological ideas of Charles Darwin about 'the survival of the fittest', and preached that the entire life of a nation must be organized and directed towards defeating its rivals either in commercial rivalry or war.

Nationalism could extend beyond the bounds of the nation state and become a form of racialism. The British looked to the self-governing dominions and America and dreamed of an Anglo-Saxon leadership of the world; the Germans of Austria and of Germany proper saw German civilization as threatened by the Slavs of the east; the Russians and their fellow Slavs in the Balkans perceived a common 'pan-Slav' destiny.

Against the background of such a climate of opinion, the cabinets of Europe pursued their dangerous rivalries. Mutual fear between states and alliances bred an arms race that bore more and more heavily on national budgets because of the ever-faster pace of technological change, rendering weapons and ships out of date within a few years of construction, and unimaginably increasing the destructiveness of war, if war should ever come.

Yet the European tensions before 1914 lay not only between nation states but also within them. Beneath the outward pomp and power of monarchies, beneath too the sober, stuffy, prosperous pattern of middle-class life, fermented the discontents of the masses. The class war cut across the prevailing nationalism. In Russia in 1906 a revolution had been repressed with difficulty by the Tsar. In Germany the working-class Social Democrats now formed the largest single party in the Reichstag, the German parliament. In France a wave of revolutionary and often violent strikes took place between 1906 and 1910, and were ruthlessly suppressed by the authorities. In Britain there had been similar fierce industrial unrest. In November 1910 a South Wales coalminers' strike had erupted into violence at Tonypandy, and the Chief Constable of Glamorgan called for the help of troops. In 1911 there were a seamen's strike, a carmen's strike and dock strikes. In Liverpool troops opened fire, killing two people, before rioting could be quelled. The very next day a rail strike began; at Llanelli the troops opened fire again, causing two more casualties. In 1912 came a national coal strike and a London dock strike. In 1913 the number of strikes and the total of union membership rose to a peak. In April 1914 the Miners' Federation, the National Union of Railwaymen and the Transport Workers' Federation formed the 'Triple Alliance', which some people feared might presage a revolutionary general strike in the near future.

In Britain there was internal violence too from an unexpected quarter – the women of the suffragette movement. Unable to persuade Asquith's Liberal government to grant women the parliamentary vote, the suffragettes resorted to such means of pressure as breaking windows, setting fire to letter-boxes and buildings, cutting telephone wires and vandalizing symbols of male supremacy such as golf greens. In 1913, in the most sensational of all suffragette gestures, Emily Davidson threw herself to her death under the hooves of the King's horse while it was running in the Derby at Epsom.

Yet the most dangerous threat to the internal stability of the United Kingdom came not from class or sex conflict, but from a dissident nationalism. The Roman Catholic majority population of Ireland renewed their old demand for Home Rule in place of government from Westminster. In 1912 the Liberal government, dependent on Irish Nationalist votes in the House of Commons, introduced a Home Rule Bill, so beginning two years of bitter strife with a Conservative and Unionist opposition that was resolved to kill or delay the bill. The Protestant minority population in Ireland prepared to fight rather than accept rule by a Dublin government –

and they were encouraged by Conservative leaders in England. By
the spring of 1914 the Ulster Volunteers, an unofficial Protestant
militia, armed with smuggled weapons, had grown into a formidable force, as had the rival Catholic Irish Volunteers. By June the
parliamentary struggle over Home Rule and the danger of civil war
in Ireland were both rising to their climax.

Nevertheless, it was to the Austro-Hungarian Empire that the
national aspirations of a subject race posed the most mortal threat.
For Austria-Hungary was an anachronism, a multi-racial state in
an age of neurotic nationalism. No logic held together this empire
of differing races and cultures; only history, which had placed
them one by one under the rule of the House of Habsburg. For
50 years the Habsburg monarchy had therefore been growing
weaker, its internal contradictions propelling it towards eventual
disintegration. Of all the nationalist movements working to
break up this ancient state, none was more dangerous than that
which wanted to unite her new South Slav provinces of Bosnia
and Herzegovina into a greater Serbia. And, as the Austrian
government rightly suspected, this movement was supported and
encouraged from the neighbouring state of Serbia. So it was
that among the crowds waiting to greet the Archduke Franz

Opposite: **Europe in 1914 before the outbreak of war**. Prior to 1914 France, Germany,
Austria-Hungary and Russia dominated Europe. The allied central powers of Germany
and Austria-Hungary were joined by Bulgaria and the Turkish Empire. Countries with
alliances against these central powers were Russia, France, Great Britain, Belgium
Serbia and Montenegro. At the outbreak of war Italy declared neutrality, having been
allied to the central powers, but later joined the Allies. Greece, Albania, Romania,
Portugal, Japan and the United States were also to join in on the Allied side.

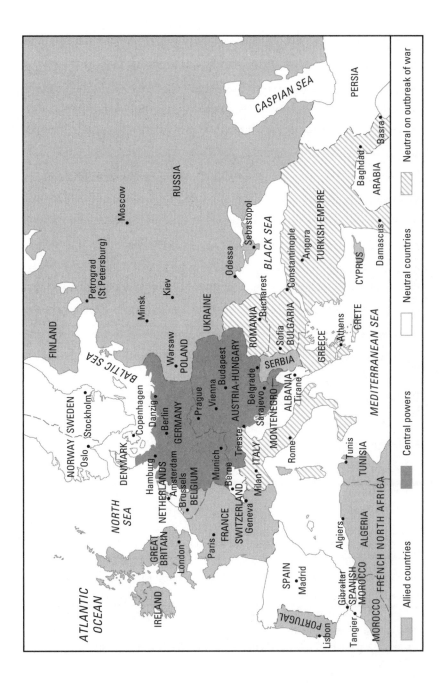

Ferdinand, heir to the Habsburg throne, and his wife in Sarajevo on that Sunday, 28 June 1914, were nationalist Slav terrorists of the Black Hand Society. One threw a bomb at the royal car on its way to the town hall, but wounded only two officers, one seriously, in a following vehicle. After an exchange of formal speeches with the burgomaster at the town hall, the Archduke and his wife drove off to visit the seriously wounded officer in hospital. As their car was passing along the quay beside the river, a young student, Gavrilo Princip, Serbian by race but Austrian by nationality, fired three shots from a pistol at close range. The Archduke and his wife died within 15 minutes. From these three shots and two deaths the violence was to ripple outwards across Europe and then the world in a conflict so terrible, so gigantic, that men were to remember it, very simply, as 'The Great War'.

•

IN VIENNA THE AUSTRIAN CHANCELLOR, Count Leopold von Berchtold, and the Chief of the General Staff, Count Franz Conrad von Hötzendorf, were at one in believing that the Archduke's assassination provided the perfect pretext for stopping, once and for all, Serbia's stirring up of Austria-Hungary's South Slav subjects; indeed, a final opportunity to restore Austria-Hungary's prestige and halt her slide into disintegration. They wished therefore to force a war on Serbia and smash her. However, behind Serbia stood Russia, self-appointed protector of all Slavs and a long-standing rival of Austria in the Balkans. Before sending Serbia an ultimatum, the Austrian Emperor therefore consulted his powerful ally the German Kaiser. Germany could have held

Austria back; instead she gave her the go-ahead. This was partly because the unstable Kaiser was in one of his bellicose moods, partly because German diplomacy felt it could not abandon Germany's only ally; partly again because the German Chief of Staff, Helmuth von Moltke, had agreed with Hötzendorf at a meeting on 12 May that, for purely military reasons, it would be better for Germany and Austria to fight a European war sooner rather than later.

Europe was divided into two armed camps glowering at each other in mutual fear – the Triple Alliance of Germany, Austria-Hungary and Italy, and the Triple Entente of France, Russia and Britain. Germany's own clumsy and bullying diplomacy, allied to her formidable industrial and military strength, had caused France and Russia to draw together in mutual support, while her challenge to British mastery of the sea had alienated Britain too. In 1913 France, with a population of only 39 million against Germany's 65 million, had lengthened the period of conscription from two to three years; her ally Russia was in the process of building strategic railways towards Germany's eastern frontier. In a year or so, Moltke and Hötzendorf feared, the military balance would have swung decisively in favour of the Entente powers.

Assured of German backing, Austria-Hungary presented an ultimatum to Serbia on 23 July, giving her 48 hours to accept humiliating terms that would infringe her sovereignty. Nevertheless, Serbia returned a submissive answer that the Kaiser himself described as 'a capitulation of the most humiliating character'. But on 28 July Austria-Hungary, determined on punishing Serbia, broke off diplomatic relations and ordered part mobilization for a local war against Serbia. Now the crisis had really broken.

The next move, the next choice of action, lay with Serbia's friend and protector Russia. While she did not wish to see Serbia smashed, or herself suffer humiliation at Austrian hands, she was all too well aware that alongside Austria-Hungary stood Germany. The Tsar favoured a partial mobilization of the Russian army, which would warn the Austrians without alarming Germany. But Russian military leaders argued that plans existed for full mobilization only, and that to order partial mobilization must lead to dislocation. On 31 July Russia ordered general mobilization; so too did Austria-Hungary. Now it was Germany's move, Germany's choice.

But Germany's long-matured military plan in fact left her government with no room for choice. Germany had faced the danger of a war on two fronts ever since France and Russia concluded their alliance in 1894. In 1905 the Chief of the General Staff, Count Schlieffen, drew up the final and perfected version of a daring plan that gambled on defeating both enemies outright within six weeks. Leaving only scanty covering forces facing the slow-mobilizing Russians, Germany would throw almost the whole of her field army against France through Holland and Belgium, outflanking the French frontier defences and surrounding the French army. With France defeated, the German forces would

Opposite: Text of the ultimatum delivered to the German government on 4 August 1914 by Sir Edward Goschen, the British Ambassador in Berlin, on the instructions of Sir Edward Grey, the Foreign Secretary. With the expiry of the ultimatum at midnight (German time), the British Empire was at war with Germany.

Sir Edward Goschen has been informed by Sir
Edward Grey that His Majesty The King of the
Belgians has addressed to His Majesty King
George an appeal for diplomatic intervention on
behalf of Belgium.

His Majesty's Government are also informed
that a Note has been delivered to the Belgian
Government by the German Government proposing
friendly neutrality entailing free passage
through Belgian territory and promising to
maintain at the conclusion of peace the
independence and integrity of the Kingdom and
its possessions, threatening to treat Belgium as
an enemy in case of refusal. It was requested
that an answer might be returned within twelve
hours.

His Majesty's Government also understand
that this request has been categorically refused
by Belgium as a flagrant violation of the Law
of Nations.

Sir Edward Grey states that His Majesty's
Government are bound to protest against this
violation of a Treaty to which Germany is a
party in common with themselves and that they
must request an assurance that the demand made
upon Belgium will not be proceeded with and that
Germany will respect the neutrality of Belgium.

Sir Edward Goschen is instructed to ask for
an immediate reply.

BERLIN, August 4, 1914.

be sent east by rail to smash the Russians in turn. The entire strategy depended on speed. This meant that the moment Russia announced mobilization, Germany must mobilize too – and more than mobilize, proceed without delay to carry out the Schlieffen Plan. Germany was therefore the only great power in the summer crisis of 1914 whose mobilization automatically meant that war must follow. More than that, the Schlieffen Plan, with its opening offensive in the West, meant that a quarrel between Germany and Russia must immediately involve France, whether or not France herself decided to honour her alliance with Russia. More than that again, Moltke had altered the Schlieffen Plan in such a way that it now carried a heavy risk of drawing Britain into the war as well.

For instead of invading Holland in order to win space for the German advance, German assault forces were to seize the vital communications bottlenecks in Luxembourg and around Liège in Belgium, even though Germany as well as Britain stood as a guarantor of Belgian neutrality under a treaty of 1839.

Thus Berlin was the hub round which the final catastrophe revolved, and at greater and greater speed. On 1 August Germany ordered general mobilization and declared war on Russia, that country having failed to comply with a German demand to cease her own mobilization. France and Belgium also mobilized that day. On 2 August Germany demanded from Belgium free passage for her troops through Belgian territory. On 3 August Belgium rejected this demand; Germany and France declared war on each other; and the British Cabinet learned that German troops were already in Luxembourg. This news and the now clearly impending German violation of Belgium as well proved decisive in terms of British policy. Britain was in no way formally committed to go to war alongside France; the Entente Cordiale had never become a full alliance. Strong elements in the Liberal Cabinet and Party had therefore been urging that Britain should stay out of a purely European power struggle. In fact secret military agreements between the British and French general staffs and a naval agreement in 1912, whereby Britain undertook to protect the French Channel coast in time of war, constituted a moral obligation hardly less strong than an alliance; a moral obligation that the despairing French ambassador in London, Paul Cambon, began to believe Britain was going to dishonour. The German invasion of Luxembourg and impending violation of Belgian neutrality enabled Herbert Asquith, the Prime Minister, and Sir Edward Grey, the Foreign Secretary, to win over all but two dissenters in the Cabinet to a war in defence of the public law of Europe and the rights of small nations. That day, 3 August, in the House of Commons, Bonar Law, leader of the Conservative and Unionist Opposition, and John Redmond, leader of the Irish Nationalist MPs, pledged full support. On 4 August, Bank Holiday Monday in England, the Prime Minister announced to the Commons that German troops had invaded Belgium; that the German government had asked Britain to condone this action in return for an undertaking not to annex Belgian territory; but that Britain had answered with an ultimatum expiring at midnight (German time) which demanded that Germany guarantee Belgian neutrality or the two countries would be at war.

In Berlin the German Chancellor, Theobald von Bethmann-Hollweg, remarked to the British ambassador: 'Just for the sake of

TWO
To win a quick victory

WAR HAD BEEN DECLARED, but the armies had yet to march. First came mobilization and deployment, lasting a fortnight or more; a titanic administrative task, planned by the general staffs of Europe for decades. In those first weeks of August several million men passed through the barracks, exchanging civilian clothes for rough new serge and hard new boots, drawing rifles and equipment, and marched off to entraining stations. Following detailed timetables, the railways rolled the armies towards the frontiers to meet each other in battle. The women and children and old men cheered the soldiers away; the soldiers leaned laughing out of carriages that bore chalked slogans like 'To Berlin' or 'To Paris'.

Behind the frontiers the units of each armed mass slotted into place: companies, battalions, brigades, divisions, army corps and armies. They reflected a Europe in transition from a life based on agriculture to one based on industrial technology. Precision engineers had designed and made the machine gun and the quick-firing field gun such as the French 75. The heavy artillery, especially the Krupp 420-millimetre and Skoda 305-millimetre siege how-itzers, was the product of the metallurgical scientist and giant steel industries. A chemical industry developed in the last 40 years supplied the explosives and the smokeless powder that propelled the shells and bullets. A new invention, the radio, supplemented the telephone and telegraph, each cumbersome set filling a horse-drawn cart. Airpower too was making its debut in war, each army deploying flimsy machines for reconnaissance; Germany had her giant airships too, the 'Zeppelins' named after their creator. The recently dawned age of the internal-combustion engine was repre-sented by staff cars, motor cycles and a relatively small number of motor trucks. Yet, once away from the railheads, the armies would depend for movement, like their predecessors through history, on hooves and feet. The farms of Europe yielded up millions of horses to haul supply wagons and ambulances, to pull the field guns and their limbers, and mount the cavalry. And – except for the small all-professional British army, which drew the bulk of its recruits from industrial towns – the majority of the rank and file came from the farms as well; tough peasants inured to hardship, jealous of their land.

Almost all pre-war thinkers had agreed that the war would be short, decided in the first great encounter battles. Only a Polish banker named Jean de Bloch, in his book *Is War Now Impossible?*, had predicted a long war of attrition fought by armies locked into trench systems. Each general staff had therefore planned to win a quick victory. The Austrians meant to crush the Serbs and then join their German ally in smashing the Russians. The Russians intended to advance on Berlin via East Prussia, while their ally France was defeating the bulk of the German army. The French, under their Plan 17 (the 17th annual revision) proposed to attack across the Franco-German frontier into Lorraine with all forces united 'whatever the circumstances', and shoulder their way to the Rhine in a phalanx of four armies. The British Expeditionary Force (known as the BEF), by pre-war arrangement, deployed south of Maubeuge, near the Belgian frontier, ready to advance as part of the flank guard on the left of the French offensive. And the Germans had the Schlieffen Plan. Seven German armies, together 1,500,000 men, the most enormous attacking array ever seen in history, were to advance against the French, while only a single army was left to face the Russians in the east. Five of these armies were to carry out a vast wheeling movement, pivoting on Verdun, that would sweep through Belgium, completely outflanking the powerful defences along the Franco-German frontier; down to the River Seine, which would be crossed west of Paris, and then swing eastwards to corral the French forces against their own frontier defences. The French, constantly outflanked and finally taken in the rear, would be certain to face total destruction.

First the gate to the Belgian plain, Liège and its circle of 12 forts, must be unlocked so that Kluck's First Army of 320,000 men, the outermost army in the German line, could pass through. On August, when mobilization had hardly begun, a special German assault force tried to take Liège by a *coup de main*. But General Gérard Leman, the fortress commander, was determined to resist to the end. The guns in the steel cupolas of the subterranean forts

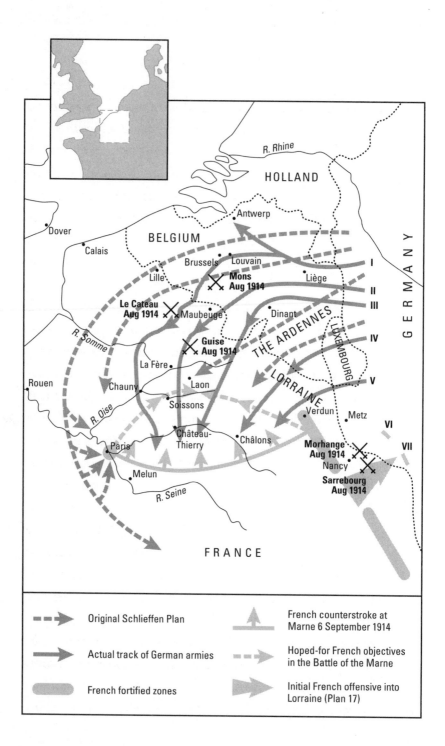

HOLLAND

BELGIUM

GERMANY

LUXEMBOURG

THE ARDENNES

LORRAINE

FRANCE

R. Rhine

Antwerp

Dover

Calais

Brussels   Louvain

Lille   Liège

Mons Aug 1914

Le Cateau Aug 1914   Maubeuge

Dinant

Guise Aug 1914

La Fère

Laon

Chauny

Soissons

Rouen

R. Somme

R. Oise

Verdun   Metz

Château-Thierry   Châlons

Paris

Melun

R. Seine

Morhange Aug 1914

Nancy

Sarrebourg Aug 1914

I
II
III
IV
V
VI
VII

- - -▶ Original Schlieffen Plan

——▶ Actual track of German armies

▬▬▬ French fortified zones

⬆ French counterstroke at Marne 6 September 1914

- - ▶ Hoped-for French objectives in the Battle of the Marne

▶ Initial French offensive into Lorraine (Plan 17)

and the rifles and machine guns of the Belgian infantry in between shattered the first German attacks in a terrible demonstration of what modern firepower could do to brave men. On 10 August the Germans brought up their heavy Krupp and Skoda siege mortars, crushing the Belgian forts one by one like beetles. The last fell on the 16th, the day German mobilization and deployment were completed. Two days later Kluck's First Army set off towards Brussels, trampling over the Belgian army's gallant but unavailing resistance.

On 14 August the French had begun their own advance under Plan 17 across the Franco-German frontier into Lorraine. Before the war French military theorists had preached that brave infantry could overcome the firepower of the defence by sheer élan and *cran* (guts). The French therefore lacked heavy mobile artillery, while their field artillery had been taught to *support* the infantry's onward rush, not prepare the way for it. Now, in red trousers and blue coats, with bugles blaring and colours flying, the French army tried to fulfil this romantic military dream. The wooded, broken hills of Lorraine provided the Germans with perfect defensive country. Day by day well-sited machine guns and artillery slaughtered the advancing French. On 19–20 August, in the twin battles of Morhange-Saarburg, Plan 17 finally broke down, for all the courage of French officers who, leading their men to the charge, 'thought it chic to die in white gloves'.

By now the Schlieffen Plan was fast unfolding. On the 20th Kluck's field-grey columns trudged for hour upon hour through

Opposite: **The Schlieffen Plan** and **the Battle of the Marne, 1914.**

the Belgian capital of Brussels before swinging southwest towards the French frontier. Behind them the German troops left a trail of atrocity – burned villages, shot civilians. On the 25th they set ablaze the ancient city of Louvain with its priceless library of medieval manuscripts. At Dinant on 23 August von Hausen's Saxons shot over 600 men, women and children in the main square. The atrocities were supposed to serve a purpose – to crush any spirit of resistance among the hapless Belgians. Instead they roused the anger of Germany's enemies, and besmirched Germany's name before the world.

For General Joseph Joffre, the French Commander-in-Chief, the cumulative signs of the enormous strength of the German right wing and its extent so far westwards were alarming indeed. Joffre reckoned that since the enemy was strong on his two flanks in Lorraine and Belgium, he must be weak in his centre, in the Ardennes. He decided to hew the German wheeling arm off at the joint by attacking here. On 22 August this French offensive too collapsed in bloody loss under the impact of German heavy and light howitzer fire. The Germans had made themselves strong everywhere by employing reservist divisions in the line, contrary to French practice. As General Charles Lanrezac's French Fifth Army was forced back from the town of Charleroi by the weight of two German armies, and Kluck's First Army curled round Lanrezac's flank and headed for the British Expeditionary Force, the appalling danger to the left of the whole Allied line became apparent.

Field-Marshal Sir John French, the British Commander-in-Chief, was actually proposing on 23 August to continue his advance in conformity with previous French plans when his liaison officer with Lanrezac arrived to tell him that his French neighbour was in full retreat. So instead the BEF prepared to fight a defensive battle against Kluck amid the slagheaps and red-brick mining villages south of Mons.

Kluck himself had no idea of the exact whereabouts of the British because his reconnoitring cavalry had been unable to penetrate the skilful British cavalry screen. Instead of outflanking the heavily outnumbered British on their left, he blundered into mounting a piecemeal frontal attack on one of the two British corps. The 23rd was a Sunday; all over the coming battlefield the church bells were summoning the devout to Mass as the British army prepared for its first battle on European soil since Waterloo. It was a day when more peacetime illusions were shed. At least one German reservist had expected the British to be dressed in bearskins and scarlet; instead he saw 'a man in a grey-brown uniform, no, in a grey-brown golfing suit with a flat-topped cloth cap. Could this be a soldier?' The Germans soon learned. Deployed behind the Mons-Condé canal, each infantryman getting off up to 15 aimed shots a minute, the superbly trained all-regular British stopped the German mass attacks in their tracks. The following day, with Kluck at last swinging wide round its left flank and the French on its right in full retreat, the BEF slipped away. It was the beginning of 'the Retreat from Mons'; a retreat interrupted only by another successful defensive time-winning battle at Le Cateau on 26 August.

Now the full weight of the German swinging arm was felt all the way from Flanders to Lorraine. With the Allied armies stumbling back in disarray, the Schlieffen Plan seemed to be fulfilling every hope of its inventor.

•

ONLY ON THE EASTERN FRONT had German calculations gone astray, for the Russians had sprung a surprise: far from being so slow to mobilize that Germany would have time to defeat France first, they began to invade East Prussia on 17 August. Their First Army under Pavel Rennenkampf (a general of German extraction) lumbered through the dense conifer forests and bleak meres of the Masurian Lakes region towards Königsberg, taking Gumbinnen and Insterburg. Further to the southwest the Russian Second Army under Alexander Samsonov advanced on Allenstein. The trim Teutonic townships of East Prussia trembled with an ancient fear of Slav hordes pouring out of the barbaric east. German roads too began to carry their sad burden of refugees. On 20 August, Maximilian von Prittwitz, commander of the heavily outnumbered German Eighth Army, lost his nerve and telephoned Moltke to say that he was ordering the abandonment of East Prussia and a general retreat behind the Vistula. That day too Moltke learned that the Austrians, who had invaded Serbia on the 12th, had been flung back by the Serbs with heavy loss; a tragicomic denouement to Austria's eagerness to force a war on Serbia during the July crisis.

To replace Prittwitz, Moltke called out of retirement the 68-year-old Paul von Hindenburg, giving him General Erich Ludendorff, a restless, aggressive soldier, as his Chief of Staff. On 23 August, the day of Mons, they arrived at Eighth Army headquarters at Marienburg, only to discover that Colonel Max Hoffmann, the able operations officer, had devised a daring plan for destroying both Russian armies – a plan that they immediately approved for action.

Samsonov's Second Army, its 200,000 men lacking field kitchens in a country of barren heath and forest, was crawling wearily forward under a broiling sun towards Allenstein – and getting further and further out of touch with Rennenkampf's First Army over to its right. Thanks to Russian indiscretion in using the radio *en clair* without enciphering, the German command enjoyed an accurate picture of enemy dispositions. Leaving only a single cavalry division facing the sluggish Rennenkampf, they concentrated their entire available strength by rail against Samsonov. On 26 August Hindenburg and Ludendorff struck home at Tannenberg, their troops utterly outfighting the bewildered, hungry and tired Russian peasant mass. By the 30th they had gained one of the great victories of history, taking 120,000 prisoners and completely destroying Samsonov's army. Samsonov shot himself in the depths of a wood. The German command now began to switch their forces against Rennenkampf.

Far away to the south, on the other side of the vast salient where Russian Poland jutted westwards between East Prussia and Austria, Conrad von Hötzendorf, the Austrian Chief of Staff, had been attacking too, driving up from eastern Galicia towards Lublin in the hope of cutting Russian communications. The force spread out along a 175-mile front. At Kraśnik on 23–26 August and Komarów on the 26th the Austrians won encouraging successes.

So, as the last days of August spun away in a roar of gunfire and an anguish of fatigue and exhaustion, the Allied armies were floundering back on both Eastern and Western Fronts. The war moved towards a climax.

•

ON GENERAL JOFFRE, the French Commander-in-Chief, the pressures were crushing. His own plans had collapsed; his impressionable troops were dismayed and discouraged by seemingly endless retreating; his liaison officer with the BEF told him – wrongly – that the British had shot their bolt. Yet Joffre, a man as massive in character as in build, did not buckle. Realizing now the full shape and purpose of the Schlieffen Plan, he ordered the formation of a new army, the Sixth, under General Michel Maunoury, to the west of the BEF, and began sending troops by rail from his now quiescent right wing in Lorraine to his ever more endangered left.

In spite of their relentless forward marching, all was not well on the German side. The Schlieffen Plan was proving too grandiose for available communications to sustain. Shrewd demolition of key railway tunnels by the Belgians had created crippling bottlenecks. Starved of reinforcements, the German armies could no longer man the extended front demanded by the Plan. Gaps opened between them. On 29 August General Lanrezac's French Fifth Army exploited such a gap to drive Karl von Bülow's Second Army back across the Oise at Guise. Even though the setback was temporary, it caused Kluck to swing inwards to help Bülow. Kluck's new southeasterly axis of advance would take him to the east of Paris instead of the *west,* as called for by the Schlieffen Plan. The shortage of men was forcing all the German armies to close up on each other; Kluck's change of direction would have been inevitable sooner or later.

Still the Germans came on under a blazing August sun, boots worn through, men swaying with fatigue; still the Allies were going back and back, and the kilometres on the signposts to Paris shrank. On 2 September the French government left Paris for Bordeaux; nevertheless, the Paris fortress commander, General Joseph Gallieni, had orders to defend the city stone by stone. Next day Kluck's First Army and Bülow's Second crossed the Marne heading southeast. Meanwhile, Kluck's right flank, the end of the German line, passed east of the Paris fortress area. Kluck's position and direction of march were observed and reported by British and French aircraft. On 4 September both Moltke, poring over his maps in his new headquarters in Luxembourg, and Joffre, sitting astride a hard chair in the dusty yard of a school at Bar-sur-Aube that now housed his headquarters, read the strategic situation alike. The German armies, far from outflanking the Allies as intended by Schlieffen, had now exposed their own flank. At 10 p.m. that evening Joffre issued his orders for an Allied counter-offensive to begin on 6 September.

THREE
The coming of stalemate

THE DAY OF 5 SEPTEMBER 1914 saw the pendulum of war swinging slowly to a momentary pause. The German armies in the west trod out the last few weary kilometres of the Schlieffen Plan; Kluck on the extreme right wing was now well south of the Marne and heading for the Seine. Feet blistered raw, in a trance of fatigue, the soldiers in the German ranks were kept going only by the prospect of victory so near. And, indeed, victory was close enough now – only 28 miles ahead of Kluck's advanced guards lay the key railway junction of Melun. If that fell, the French armies would be virtually severed from the rest of the country. Yet a curious electric unease ran through the German ranks, 'for no special reason', wrote a reserve officer in the First Army, 'other than such as losing touch with Bülow's Second Army, or the apparent complete absence of communications behind, or the news gradually trickling through to us that our artillery was running short of ammunition'. The Allied armies, however, had had no vision of victory to sustain them during the long retreat from the frontiers. Joffre was only too well aware that further setbacks might easily carry his volatile French soldiers over the edge of moral collapse. Even to the phlegmatic professionals of the BEF, the last fortnight seemed like six weeks. 'They were very glum,' wrote a British staff officer, 'they marched silently, doggedly, never a whistle or a song, or even a ribald jest, to help weary feet along the road.'

Moltke had ceded the priceless German moral advantage before the Battle of the Marne was even joined, before Joffre had issued his own orders for the Allied counterstroke. On 4 September he finally abandoned the Schlieffen Plan by ordering his right-flank armies to stand fast, their new task 'to act against any operations of the enemy from the neighbourhood of Paris'. Instead he now looked for victory in a concentric attack by his left-wing armies on the French defences east of Verdun. Unfortunately, Moltke was so out of touch with reality that for the First Army to 'stand fast' in the position indicated by him meant a two days' retreat. On 6 September, as this retreat by the First Army coincided with the Allied forward movement on the first day of the Battle of the Marne, the German spirit plummeted: 'Why? we were all asking – why were we going back?' Allied spirits soared: 'The happiest day in my life; we marched towards the morning sun,' wrote a BEF colonel in his diary.

Joffre's plan was simple but grandiose: while the two French armies along the southern face of the German bulge held firm, the flank armies near the Paris and Verdun fortress areas would drive in the bulge's sides. If these flank armies could thrust fast enough and deep enough into the German rear, the invader might not merely be stopped, but destroyed. The first day of the battle was not promising however. Maunoury's Sixth Army, attacking the German flank east of Paris, was stopped with heavy loss by Kluck's First Army. The BEF, a day's march behind its neighbouring armies, had not yet got into the fight. On the 7th and 8th Kluck forced Maunoury on to the defensive, while the BEF made only hesitant progress against a resolute and skilful defence in the intricate, stream-cut countryside south of the Marne. After three days Joffre's counterstroke had proved not so much a smashing blow as a slow, fumbling and confused forward movement that in places had been stopped and thrown back.

There was one dangerous development from the German point of view. Kluck, swinging back the First Army's front from south to east in order to face Maunoury, had left a gap between himself and Bülow covered only by a thin screen of all arms. Into this gap the BEF and part of the French Fifth Army were slowly plodding. Moltke, far away in Luxembourg, feared that Kluck might be cut off and destroyed. Moltke was in any case a spent man, his nerve in shreds. About this time a staff officer found him 'sitting hunched up over his table, his face buried in both hands. Moltke looked up and turned a pale and tear-stained face on the officer.' Instead of a will to win that matched the performance of his troops in the field, Moltke gave way to despair; and in this contrast with Joffre's massive personal strength lay the key to the issue of the Battle of the Marne. On 9 September Moltke sent a

Opposite: **The Eastern Front 1914–17.**

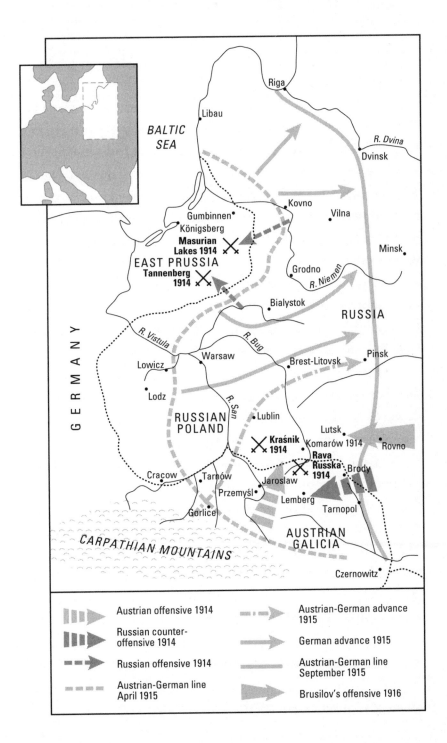

Legend:

- Austrian offensive 1914
- Russian counter-offensive 1914
- Russian offensive 1914
- Austrian-German line April 1915
- Austrian-German advance 1915
- German advance 1915
- Austrian-German line September 1915
- Brusilov's offensive 1916

senior staff officer, Colonel Richard Hentsch, to assess the situation at the headquarters of the German right-wing armies, with full powers to give orders in his name. Hentsch first visited Bülow at Second Army; and Bülow, old and steeped in peacetime war-gaming, urged that a retreat behind the Marne was the only way to avoid a catastrophe. Hentsch agreed. At First Army headquarters he ordered Kluck to abandon his attacks on Maunoury and to fall back northeastwards behind the Marne in order to link up again with Bülow. The Battle of the Marne had been decided – without the German armies being decisively beaten on the ground. A commander more resolute and energetic than Moltke might still have won because reinforcements lay near enough at hand. On 7 September the French fortress of Maubeuge fell, releasing the German Seventh Reserve Corps. This corps could have been deployed in the fatal gap between Kluck and Bülow by late on 9 September. Instead it was sent to Flanders.

Between 9 and 13 September the field-grey masses ebbed back to the Aisne, only sluggishly pursued by the exhausted Allied troops; a glum retreat, often in heavy rain: 'no jokes, no complaints, just a bitter indifference'. In the euphoria of advancing, some Allied officers expected to be on German soil in a matter of weeks. The enemy stood behind the Aisne and fought on the immensely strong natural position of the Chemin des Dames Ridge. On 13 September the BEF and the French Fifth Army, counting on easily breaking through, attacked up the steep, winding valleys that led to the crest. However, the German Seventh Reserve Corps arrived after a march of 40 miles in 24 hours, just in time to block the British First Corps under General

Sir Douglas Haig, which had even reached the crest of the ridge at one point. A ferocious 'soldiers' battle' now developed, with local attack and counter-attack amid the wooded re-entrants and steep spurs above the Aisne. The face of future warfare on the Western Front began dimly to show itself: primitive trenches; artillery spotting and direction by aircraft or balloons; the gruesome losses sustained even by skilled professionals like the BEF when attacking in the teeth of enemy bombardment; mud, thanks to the continuous rain that had replaced the roasting sunshine of August and the first week of September. Both sides fed in fresh forces, striving to throw the other back; neither succeeded. At the beginning of October the Battle of the Aisne petered out in deadlock. However, between the Aisne front and the Channel there still lay an open flank. The German and Allied high commands looked to that flank in fresh hopes of a victory.

•

ON THE EASTERN FRONT, TOO, initial plans for winning the war at a blow had foundered as the armies marched and manoeuvred over the wide dusty plains. After their successes at Kraśnik and Komarów in the last week of August, the Austro-Hungarian armies had seemed about to encircle and destroy the Russian Fifth Army. Owing to muddled decisions taken by Hötzendorf, the Austrian Chief of Staff, at the time of mobilization, the Austrian forces in Galicia were some 15 divisions weaker than they need have been. As a result, their undermanned right flank was driven in by a Russian counterstroke led by General Aleksei Brusilov, who was to emerge as one of the ablest generals of the war.

Under the shock of defeat the Austro-Hungarian ranks dissolved in panic. The great Austrian fortress of Lemberg fell, endangering the communications of the Austrian forces still thrusting northwards. Hötzendorf, a fantasist given to inventing grand Napoleonic manoeuvres off the map, now ordered the Russian westward thrust to be attacked from north and south. This demanded an agility and drive on the part of his armies that was quite beyond their fighting capabilities and the slipshod Austrian staff work. By 11 September even Hötzendorf had to recognize that he was threatened by catastrophe and order a general retreat. So the Austrians in the east fell back behind the River San, while in the west their German allies were falling back to the Aisne. In Galicia, as in France, the sun and dust of August had yielded to rain and mud. 'Day and night,' recorded the Austrian official history later, 'behind a huge train of transport vehicles marched the infantry, with bowed heads...the artillery, sinking in up to their axles in the morass that the roads became...the cavalry regiments, like horsemen of the Apocalypse, in molten confusion, made their way on, their presence palpable from afar by the penetrating smell of the festering galls of hundreds of led horses.' In pursuit of his dream of a gigantic victory, Hötzendorf had lost 350,000 men out of 900,000 and inflicted a wound on the morale of his multi-racial army from which it would never really recover.

Yet the day that Lemberg fell to the Russians also saw the Russian invasion of East Prussia finally collapse when the German Eighth Army pursued the wreckage of Rennenkampf's First Army across the Russian frontier. On 7 September Hindenburg and Ludendorff had attacked Rennenkampf in a strong position amid the Masurian Lakes with his right flank on the Baltic coast. While part of the Eighth Army assaulted the entrenched Russian troops frontally, a flanking group under General Hermann von François smashed northwards through a one-mile gap between two lakes into the Russian left. On 9–10 September, just as the Battle of the Marne was reaching its denouement, Rennenkampf abandoned his defences and fell back in dire confusion. Although he managed to escape the complete catastrophe suffered by Samsonov at Tannenberg, he lost 125,000 men in the Battle of the Masurian Lakes, and his army struggled back across the frontier on the 13th with its morale in its worn-out boots.

On every front and for every belligerent great power the bright hopes of August lay trampled in the rains of September. Yet fresh hope already beckoned the armies on; the general staffs studied their maps and planned new offensives that might yet bring victory in 1914.

•

FROM THE OUTSET OF THE BATTLE OF THE AISNE Joffre had intended to couple a wide outflanking movement with his frontal attack. When this move was blocked by newly arrived German formations, Joffre repeated his swing further north – only to be blocked yet again. By the first week of October, as each side sought to outflank the other but instead kept colliding, the struggle had reached the rolling downland around Arras. Although German heavy guns tumbled the lovely Renaissance Flemish gables of Arras into ruins, the French line held: step by step the fighting and the trenches therefore extended north towards the sea.

Meanwhile, the German battering train of heavy guns and mortars had been crushing the forts of Antwerp as they had those of Liège. On 9 October, despite the dubious assistance of a new and largely untrained 'Royal Naval Division' sent at the urging of Winston Churchill, the First Lord of the Admiralty, Antwerp surrendered. The Belgian field army escaped down the coast to join the main Allied line. Now the Western Front had reached the North Sea at Nieuport; there was no longer an open flank to turn.

Yet between the sea and Arras the line on both sides was still patchily held by troops rushed up piecemeal. Both Joffre and Erich von Falkenhayn, who had now replaced Moltke as German Chief of Staff, decided to break through before his enemy's defence could solidify.

On 12 October Joffre struck first, between Ypres and La Bassée; his aim was to recapture the industrial city of Lille and drive deep into Belgium. At the beginning the Allied forces, including the BEF (transferred to Flanders from the Aisne), seemed to do well, pushing the enemy back from the outskirts of Ypres, capturing Armentières and crossing the River Lys. Lille itself lay only some three miles distant. The advance stuck from the 18th onwards, for the Allies had run into the full weight of Falkenhayn's own offensive, aimed at breaking through to Calais. On the coastal sector from Nieuport to Dixmude the Belgians and a French marine division narrowly held on against a German attack supported by the heavy guns freed from the siege of Antwerp, but the crisis here passed when the Belgians opened the dykes and the waters rose along the Allied front. Around Arras the French, under Louis de Maudhuy, desperately resisted another powerful German onslaught. It was in the centre, between Ypres and La Bassée, that the fighting was most critical. On 29 October Falkenhayn launched a completely new formation, Group Fabeck, against the already desperately pressed Allied line in the Ypres salient. Supported by abundant artillery with plenty of shells, Fabeck attacked through fog astride the Ypres-Menin road near the village of Gheluvelt. The defending British, however, lacked heavy guns and even shells for their field guns; all depended on the musketry of the infantry. Fabeck's men were largely young volunteers fired with patriotic courage, but poorly trained and led by elderly 'dug-out' officers. The British regulars cut them down in masses. Nevertheless, sheer weight of numbers told. On 31 October the Germans broke through the British Front at Gheluvelt; there were signs of the contagion of retreat among the battle-fatigued defenders; and another prompt German blow might have brought about a general collapse. The crisis of the First Battle of Ypres had arrived. The situation was saved by one battalion, the 2nd Royal Worcestershire Regiment – the only available reserve. The Worcestershires caught the enemy off-balance in a moment of relaxation after victory and tumbled them back in rout. Although this counter-attack restored the Allied line, the fighting still went on savagely; a confused sprawl of small-scale struggles between companies, battalions and brigades for a section of primitive trench, the line of a road or wood, a farm or a village.

On 11 November came a last grand German attempt at the breakthrough. This time the volunteer corps were stiffened by the Prussian Guard Division. Although the hotch-potch of British and French units mixed together had by now been reduced to half strength or less, their fire stopped and broke up even the Guard. Only at one point, just north of the Menin road, did the German onslaught roll over the British position. Nevertheless, isolated British units held the Guard up long enough for a counter-attack to be mounted by the 52nd Light Infantry (the regiment that had successfully counter-attacked Napoleon's Imperial Guard at Waterloo). The Prussian Guard, taken by surprise, fell back, and the First Battle of Ypres died away in stalemate. The battle marked the death of the old British regular army, for 58,000 officers and men had fallen.

Now the stalemate – and the trenches – extended solidly from the North Sea to Switzerland. Such a phenomenon had never before been seen in war. Even on the Eastern Front, where the proportion of soldiers to space was so much smaller and the pendulum of advance and retreat swung over vast distances, the 1914 campaign finally came to rest in stalemate also. The Russian advance after Lemberg was held by the Austrians on the crestline of the Carpathian Mountains; a German advance on Warsaw foundered in confused and bloody battles fought in snow and bitter frost between 18 and 25 November, and petered out in the face of Russian barbed wire and trenches on 6 December. On the same day, after a three-day battle, the doughty Serbs threw back in ruin a second Austrian attempt to conquer their country. The improvised plans of autumn had followed the long-matured plans of summer to the grave: victims alike of the firepower of modern weapons. By Christmas, the time when the soldiers were once supposed to have been home in victory, the truth had sunk into every belligerent nation that this was going to be a long, grim war; and with unquenched resolve they set out to wage it and win it.

FOUR

The civilians go to war

WHILE THE SOLDIERS TOILED to transform the first shallow trenches into elaborate systems of field fortifications, and the general staffs sought a way out of a strategic dilemma they had never envisaged, governments and peoples grappled with the novel problems of mass technological war. The conflict had already passed beyond the bounds of a traditional contest between armies and become a struggle between entire societies and all their resources, human and material. The year 1915 saw the transition between the old order of peacetime and the new conditions of total war; a time of radical and often painful adaptation for military and civilians alike.

Imperial Germany now faced that very war on two fronts that the Schlieffen Plan had been intended to avert; and her only major ally, Austria, was ramshackle and inefficient. In one German officer's caustic phrase, Germany was shackled to a corpse. Yet Germany enjoyed enormous assets as Europe's greatest industrial and military power. Her steel production and her superb engineering and chemical industries were swiftly adapted to producing weapons and ammunition in abundance. The German army remained the most formidable of all armies, despite its losses in the 1914 campaign, its brain a highly professional general staff and its backbone a corps of 100,000 well-trained and resourceful non-commissioned officers. By 1915 it had learned to respect the killing power of modern weapons; it had adapted swiftly and skilfully to trench warfare, thanks to its strength in heavy mobile artillery and to equipping its infantry before the war with effective grenades, mortars and entrenching tools. Germany's position astride the heart of Europe and a spider's web of strategic railways enabled her swiftly to switch her reserves from one front to another. If the Allies were to win this war, they had to beat the German army backed by the German industrial machine and the intelligent, disciplined and patriotic German people – a formidable task.

There was no similarly predominant partner among the Allies; each had its strengths and shortcomings. Russia, still a country of primitive peasant agriculture, had the manpower; her problem lay in mobilizing and equipping it. Her industrial base was new and comparatively small. In 1915 the Tsar's government embarked on a breakneck expansion of this base in order to supply the munitions that the Russian army desperately lacked. It would be many months before this wartime industrial revolution produced guns and shells at the front, and meanwhile such frantic economic and social change was to sharpen all the existing tensions in Russian society.

For the Western Allies, Britain and France, the supreme fact of 1915 lay in the German occupation of Belgium and northern France, with the nearest German troops entrenched only 60 miles from Paris. This residue of the miscarried Schlieffen Plan was to determine the entire strategic and political pattern of the war. Whatever the strength of the German defences, whatever the weaknesses in the Allied armies, neither a French government nor the French people could tamely accept this continued occupation of their soil. To strive to throw the Germans out was therefore an imperative, overruling all other factors – just as it would have been for the British had the Germans been entrenched at Canterbury. In 1915 the burden of the offensive would fall on the French army, for the British regular army had been largely destroyed and Kitchener's 'New Army' of civilian volunteers could not be fielded en masse until 1916. The French army had already lost 855,000 killed, wounded and missing in the 1914 campaigns. Moreover, the French, expecting a short war of movement, had neglected to equip themselves with mobile heavy artillery. Now they were forced to strip the guns out of their fortresses to repair the lack; guns not always suitable in type for smashing trenches.

Britain, for her part, faced a situation entirely new in her history. For the first time she was going to have to field on the Continent, not just a small regular force but a mass army composed of citizens from all walks of life. Yet so ingrained was the traditional dislike of the European system of conscription that this new army was raised entirely by voluntary recruiting; a method which, apart from its inherent unfairness between the willing and the reluctant, left the government with no control over the speed quantities of weapons and ammunition under heavy political pressure for economy, was now called on to expand production at breakneck speed. It duly placed the orders, but firms unused to such precision work failed to deliver on time. By the spring of 1915 the British army in France was rationed to a few rounds per gun per day. The Commander-in-Chief, Sir John French, leaked the details of the shortage to *The Times* after an abortive offensive at Neuve Chapelle in March, and blamed it on the War Office. The so-called 'shell scandal' helped to bring down Asquith's Liberal government in May and bring in a coalition. In June Lloyd George became head of a new Ministry of Munitions, with the task of masterminding industrial mobilization. It was the moment when Victorian laissez-faire liberalism began to give way to State intervention in all aspects of the national life; a revolution indeed. As Lloyd George told an audience that summer:

> We are fighting against the best organized community in the world, the best organized either for peace or war, and we have been employing too much the haphazard, leisurely, go-as-you-please methods, which, believe me, would not have enabled us to maintain our place as a nation even in peace very much longer.

In all countries industrial mobilization carried in its train a social revolution – and a revolution in manners. The servant class, whether male or female, began to melt away into the forces or the munitions factories, and for the first time women took over traditional male jobs. Women bus and tram conductors appeared;

women porters and guards on the railways; middle-class girls escaped from Victorian domestic imprisonment to work in government offices. As women made the most of their new-found and well-paid freedom, the stiff decorum of pre-war middle-class life vanished, along with the corset and the pavement-length skirt. Love affairs with men so likely soon to die in battle made nonsense of Victorian ideas of female chastity. Total war was doing more to liberate women than all the efforts of feminists before 1914.

It was modern technology that most dramatically demonstrated that the old distinction between armies in the field and civilians at home was no more. In April 1915 Britain lost her ancient immunity as an island from the horrors of war, when she was attacked for the first time from the air. A German airship dropped a few bombs on East Anglian towns, the beginning of a desultory offensive through the summer. On 7 and 8 September the Zeppelins attacked London itself, capital of the Empire, killing 38 and wounding 124. The moral effect was disproportionate; soldiers home on leave found that civilians were more concerned with their trifling experiences in air raids than with hearing about the front. An even more shocking affront to British ideas of civilian immunity was administered by a German submarine on 7 May 1915, when it sank the Cunard liner *Lusitania* off the coast of Ireland with the loss of over 1,000 lives. Even though the German government had published warnings in American papers against travelling in her, and even though she was carrying a cargo of arms, her destruction caused an explosion of anti-German hatred in Britain. Shops with seemingly German names were attacked and looted. But the British were not alone in feeling a passionate hatred of the enemy coupled with an invincible sense of the righteousness of their own cause, for these were the fuel that kept every nation's war effort burning. The peoples demanded victory, and the baffled but still optimistic generals set out to win it for them.

•

FALKENHAYN, THE GERMAN CHIEF OF STAFF, at first wanted to employ his central strategic reserve in a great offensive in Flanders before the new British citizen army could arrive in strength. He believed that German chemists had provided him with the tool of the breakthrough: chlorine gas to be released from cylinders and blown over the enemy lines by a favourable breeze. The weakness of his Austrian ally in the face of a tenacious Russian offensive over the crestline of the Carpathians convinced him that he must use his reserve on the Eastern Front instead. He therefore decided to strike merely a limited blow in the west to cover the movement of troops eastwards. At 5 p.m. on 22 April 1915, after a violent bombardment of the medieval city of Ypres, a greenish-yellow cloud began to drift towards the Allied trenches on the Langemarck sector of the Ypres Salient. In its path stood Algerian and overage territorial troops of the French army. Choking in agony, panic-stricken, they broke to the rear, opening up a four-mile gap in the front. Yet the Germans, fearing to run into their own gas, were slow to follow up. The 1st Canadian Division and some British units managed to cordon off the breakthrough area in time, and the Second Battle of Ypres degenerated into just another stalemated and murderous struggle. But it had served its purpose of covering the movement of 11 first-class German divisions (including two of the Guard) to the Eastern Front.

On 2 May the German Eleventh Army and the Austrian Fourth smashed into the Russian line between Gorlice and Tarnów in Galicia. It was a new kind of offensive, planned and executed by a formidable military team: General August von Mackensen, energetic, thrusting, and Hans von Seeckt, his intellectually brilliant Chief of Staff. The attacking divisions were slotted into place with such secrecy that the Russians never guessed that an offensive was pending. The preliminary bombardment lasted only four hours – a concentrated hurricane of fire from 700 guns, half of them heavy, on an 18-mile front, smashing and dazing the Russian defence into impotence. At 10 a.m. on 2 May, under a cloudless blue sky above the open plains, the German assault forces struck. Here too there were novelties: instead of fixed linear objectives, the troops were ordered to drive on as far as possible at utmost speed. Local reserves lay close at hand, but with the task of exploiting success rather than shoring up failure. The Russian line, much less strongly fortified and held than defences on the Western Front, starved of guns and ammunition, collapsed. An eyewitness wrote: 'Here and there loam-grey figures jumped up and ran back, weaponless, in grey fur caps and fluttering unbuttoned greatcoats. Soon there was not one of them remaining. Like a flock of sheep they fled in wild confusion.'

The advance rolled through the sun and dust. By 14 May the German and Austrian advance had reached the River San, 80 miles from their start-line. The entire Russian position along the

Carpathians, taken in flank, collapsed, so ending the menace to the Austrian heartlands. On 3 June the fortress of Przemyśl fell; on 22 June Lemberg followed suit.

In July Falkenhayn swung the axis of Mackensen's offensive northwards. Warsaw fell on 4 August; Brest-Litovsk at the end of the month. Meanwhile, far in the north, Hindenburg had captured Kovno. Still the Russians retreated, all the confusions of disaster made worse by the inefficiency of Russian administration, which ensured that available supplies and munitions were rarely at the places where they were needed. The Russian infantry, ill-educated, ill-trained and ill-led, only a third of them possessing rifles, was herded up like cattle by the superbly professional German troops.

Yet for all his success, Falkenhayn did not mean to repeat Napoleon's error of driving on and on in hopes of totally defeating Russia. This he believed to be too great a gamble. His purpose was to cripple her militarily. He therefore closed his offensive down in September, by which time he had won the greatest single victory in the field ever to be gained during the Great War, advancing up to 300 miles, inflicting casualties of some 2,000,000, half of them in prisoners, and taking 3,000 guns. The blow to Russian national morale and to the prestige of the Tsarist regime was devastating. The Tsar Nicholas II responded by dismissing the Grand Duke Nicholas, the Russian Commander-in-Chief, and assuming personal command of his armies, with General Alexeiev as his Chief of Staff – an ill-judged decision, for it tied his own personal standing to the fortunes of Russian arms.

In the West Joffre, the French Commander-in-Chief, had planned for, and expected, just the kind of swift breakthrough and sweeping advance that Falkenhayn achieved in the east. Unfortunately for him and his troops, the circumstances were very different. They were not attacking a lightly fortified front thinly held by inferior troops short of firepower, but a trench zone designed, dug and defended by the best army in Europe. On 9 May Joffre launched his grand spring offensive between Lens and Arras with 18 divisions, the main blow falling on a four-mile front; his aim to drive in the western flank of the German bulge towards Paris. On the left of the French the BEF, desperately lacking guns and shells, attacked towards the Aubers Ridge. The French suffered some 100,000 casualties, the British 27,000; the ground gained was negligible.

Joffre, confidence undimmed, convincing himself that at least he was weakening the enemy by attrition, prepared an even grander autumn offensive: a double blow against the German bulge, a main thrust northwards in Champagne, coupled with a secondary eastwards thrust in Artois. Both flanks of the German bulge could collapse; the Allied advance would cut vital German communications; and the German armies would retreat from French territory. For the Champagne attack Joffre assembled 35 divisions, including 10 divisions of cavalry ready for the pursuit. In a three-day bombardment 900 heavy and 1,600 field guns would flatten a path for the infantry through the German defences. Joffre told his troops: 'Your élan will be irresistible. It will carry you in the first bound to the enemy batteries behind the fortified lines opposite you. You will give him neither respite nor rest until the victory is complete.' On 25 September, a day of rain and clinging mud, the French infantry followed the barrage with drums beating, fifes playing, 'La Marseillaise' ringing out. The bombardment, though the heaviest in the war so far, failed to smash the German defences or adequately to cut the barbed wire. Once again the firepower of a resolute defence prevailed over the onward rush of brave men. After some small initial gains the offensive degenerated as usual into a shambles of local struggles. In 10 days Joffre lost 145,000 men for no result.

In Artois the French attack at Vimy Ridge ended in outright and bloody failure. It was the British in the Battle of Loos, over-running the village of that name and advancing to the outskirts of Lens, who came nearest to success, for the Germans had not been expecting an attack. When two New Army divisions, the London Territorials and the Scottish, breached the German second line, the local German command had no immediate reserves to plug the gap. The British Commander-in-Chief, Sir John French, had kept his own reserves 16 miles behind the front instead of allotting them to Haig, the First Army commander conducting the offensive. By the time these reserves arrived and attacked, the enemy had sealed off the breach. This misjudgement doomed French, already under mounting criticism, and on 17 December he was replaced by Sir Douglas Haig, a Presbyterian Scot of rock-like determination, sanguine temperament and far greater open-mindedness than his critics like to believe.

Thus the offensives of 1915 had merely borne out at terrible cost Lord Kitchener's judgement at the very beginning of the year that 'the German lines in France may be looked on as a fortress

Below The Archduke Franz Ferdinand, heir to the throne of Austria-Hungary, leaving the town hall at Sarajevo with his wife, Sophie, a few minutes before their assassination on 28 June 1914. This event began the final crisis that led to the Great War. **Bottom** Under arrest. The figure second from the right in this photograph is believed to be the chief organizer of the assassination and the man who fired the fatal shots, Gavrilo Princip.

GREAT BRITAIN DECLARES WAR ON GERMANY.

SUMMARY REJECTION OF BRITISH ULTIMATUM.

ALL EYES ON THE NORTH SEA

INVASION OF BELGIUM.

The following announcement was issued at the Foreign Office at 12.15 a.m.:—

"Owing to the summary rejection by the German Government of the request made by His Majesty's Government for assurances that the neutrality of Belgium would be respected, His Majesty's Ambassador in Berlin has received his passports, and His Majesty's Government has declared to the German Government that a state of war exists between Great Britain and Germany as from 11 p.m. on August 4."

Huge crowds in Whitehall and Trafalgar Square greeted the news with round after round of cheers.

11 p.m. London time is midnight Berlin time, the hour at which the British ultimatum expired.

The King held a Council at midnight to sign the proclamation of war.

Great Britain had sent an ultimatum to Germany which expired at midnight.

This was due to Germany's refusal to leave Belgium neutral and her invasion of that country.

The German Ambassador went to 10, Downing Street at 12.10 a.m. to receive his papers. He looked a broken man.

Sir Edward Goschen, the British Ambassador in Berlin, demanded his passports.

Admiral Jellicoe is in command of the British Fleet.

The State has taken over all the British railways.

A German warship attacked the French port Bona, in Algeria.

The main centre of interest in the war has shifted suddenly from the French frontier to the North Sea.

A land battle is not to be expected till the process of mobilisation is complete—for several days. Fleets can act instantly, immediately after a declaration of war. The most powerful ships of all Navies are maintained in a perpetual condition of readiness.

The British and German Fleets now face one another in the North Sea.

The British ultimatum to Germany required a satisfactory answer as regards the neutrality of Belgium by midnight last night.

Germany had threatened to make a passage for her armies through Belgium on Monday night "by force of arms."

German troops yesterday actually entered Belgium.

Admiral Sir John R. Jellicoe, K.C.B., the Kitchener of the Navy, has assumed supreme command of the Home Fleets, and Rear-Admiral C. E. Madden, C.V.O., has been appointed his Chief of the Staff. Field-Marshal Sir John French has been reappointed Inspector-General of the Forces.

The strength of the main British and main German Fleets in the most powerful type of ships is as follows:

	Dreadnoughts.	Pre-Dreadnoughts.	Battle Cruisers.
British	19	8	4
German	13	5	4

Both Great Britain and Germany have also brought up large numbers of older and smaller ships.

The weight of metal from the heavy guns in the British main Fleet is superior by 60 per cent. to that in the German main Fleet.

This is due to the fact that the British Dreadnoughts carry 12in. and 13.5in. guns, whereas the German Dreadnoughts only carry 11in. and 12in. guns.

The British strength in modern destroyers ... be placed at 120 British total available is about 70 boats, and the German force is not believed to exceed 30.

The British Fleets are manned by at least 100,000 officers and men; the German Fleets by about 65,000 men.

The British Government has taken over the control of all the railways. They will be worked by a committee of general managers as one railway. The staffs will remain as before and receive orders through their own officials.

The Government is preparing a scheme to control the distribution of the country's food supplies.

£1 notes are to be put in circulation on Friday, when millions of them will be ready. Ten shilling notes will follow later.

TWO MORE BRITISH DREADNOUGHTS.

ACQUISITION FROM TURKEY.

We are officially informed that the Government have taken over the two battleships, one completed and the other shortly due for completion, which had been ordered in this country by the Turkish Government and the two destroyer leaders ordered by the Government of Chili.

The two battleships will receive the names Agincourt and Erin, and the destroyer leaders will be called Faulkner and Broke, after two famous naval officers.

The two Dreadnought battleships are:

1. The SULTAN OSMAN I. Built by Messrs. Armstrong. She is the largest battleship yet completed, being of 27,500 tons displacement. She has seven turrets, each carrying two 12in. guns. The vessel was laid down to the order of the Brazilian Government, but was taken over by Turkey for £2,723,000.

2. The RESHADIEH.—Built by Messrs. Vickers. Displacement 23,000 tons. She has ten 13.5in. guns mounted on twin turrets on the centre line as in the King George class.

SELLING THE SKIN.

From Our Parliamentary Correspondent

I hear that on Thursday the German Ambassador in London made, on behalf of the German Government, a verbal communication to Sir Edward Grey to the effect that, in the event of Great Britain remaining neutral in Germany's war with France, Germany would undertake, "when she had brought France to her knees," not to deprive France of any of her territory in Europe but to "content herself" with taking the French Colonial possessions.

HOLLAND'S FEARS.

From Our Own Correspondent.

[illegible]

HOME FLEETS.

SUPREME COMMAND.

SIR JOHN JELLICOE, K.C.B.

THE KING'S MESSAGE TO THE FLEET.

With the approval of the King, Admiral Sir John R. Jellicoe, K.C.B., K.C.V.O., has assumed supreme command of the Home Fleets, with the acting rank of Admiral; and

Rear-Admiral Charles E. Madden, C.V.O,

ADMIRAL SIR JOHN R. JELLICOE.

has been appointed to be his Chief of the Staff.

Both appointments date from yesterday.

The King has sent the following message to Admiral Sir John Jellicoe:—

At this grave moment in our national history I send to you, and through you to the officers and men of the fleets of which you have assumed command, the assurance of my confidence that under your direction they will revive and renew the old glories of the Royal Navy and prove once again the sure shield of Britain and of her Empire in the hour of trial.

GEORGE R.I.

The King's message has been communicated to the senior naval officers on all stations outside of home waters.

SIR JOHN FRENCH.

INSPECTOR-GENERAL OF THE FORCES AGAIN.

Field-Marshal Sir John French has been appointed Inspector-General of the Forces. The appointment, which dates from August 1, was announced in the *London Gazette* last night.

This office is the one Sir John French held from 1907 until 1911, when he relieved Sir William Nicholson in the office of Chief of the Imperial General Staff. He resigned the latter appointment as the result of the repudiated guarantee to General Gough in connection with the plot against Ulster.

HUGE GERMAN CREDIT.

£250,000,000 FOR WAR.

BERLIN, Tuesday.

A Bill was presented in the Reichstag to-day authorising the Imperial Chancellor to raise a credit of about £250,000,000 to meet non-recurring extraordinary expenditure.—Reuter.

7.30 a.m. EDITION.

FIRE AND SWORD IN BELGIUM

GREAT GERMAN ADVANCE.

BATTLE NEAR LIEGE.

TOWNS ABLAZE.

POPULATION CUT UP.

GERMAN AIRMAN KILLED.

FROM OUR SPECIAL CORRESPONDENT.

MAASTRICHT (in Holland, near the Belgian frontier), Tuesday Evening.

(By telephone to Amsterdam.)

The Belgian frontier town of Visé, about eight miles from Maastricht, was taken by a body of German infantry and artillery this afternoon.

An engagement took place and lasted several hours.

The retreating Belgians blew up a bridge over the Meuse, but German sappers, covered by heavy artillery fire, built a new bridge and crossed the river.

Visé is practically destroyed.

Firing occurred throughout the day and was heard in all the surrounding towns.

LIEGE FIGHTING.

From Our Own Correspondent.

BRUSSELS, Tuesday, 6 p.m.

I am informed by the War Office that Liège and its forts are defending themselves energetically.

BRUSSELS, Wednesday.

A stubborn battle has been fought on the outskirts of Liège, where 80,000 Germans attempted to force their advance across Belgium and were engaged by the Liège militia, who after a fierce encounter so harassed the German troops on the right that they were forced to retire.—Exchange Telegraph Company.

LIEGE, Tuesday.

The Germans, hindered by the destroyed bridges, viaducts, and railways, have been compelled to make for the north and have violated Dutch territory at Tilburg.

They crossed the Meuse at Eysden. The 10th army corps is said to be at Eysden, the 7th, 40,000 strong, at Verviers, and the 6th at a place unknown.

Visé and Argenteau are in flames, the Germans having set fire to them. Civilians are reported to have fired on the Germans, who are reported to have decimated the population of Visé.

A hundred thousand Germans are marching on Liège, where an attack is expected to-morrow.

A wounded German officer who was captured expressed great astonishment at the resistance which the Germans were finding in Belgium. They had been assured, he said, in Berlin that no opposition would be encountered in Belgium.

A German airman has been killed.—Reuter.

GERMANS IN GREAT FORCE.

ATTACK ALL ALONG THE FRONTIER.

From Our Own Correspondent.

PARIS, Tuesday.

News has just reached the French Government that the Germans have invaded Belgium in great force.

Numbers of men in armoured motor-cars and trains have entered the country near Visé, facing the great fortress of Liège, which dominates the Meuse valley, blowing up bridges.

The German attack is developing all along the Belgian frontier.

From Our Own Correspondent.

ROTTERDAM, Tuesday.

A correspondent of the Rotterdam *Courant* who stood on a hill at Vaals almost at the point where the frontiers of Holland, Belgium, and Germany meet, says he saw 30,000 Germans enter Belgium. The invaders issued proclamations declaring that they had come to assist Belgium, and several villagers welcomed them.

"WILL ENGLAND DELAY?"

KING ALBERT'S SUPREME APPEAL TO THE EMPIRE.

From Our Own Correspondent.

BRUSSELS, Tuesday.

King Albert was cheered to the echo to-day when he entered Parliament to address the united Chambers. His Majesty said:

"We are determined on the greatest sacrifices to defend our beloved country. David has faced Goliath. In the last twenty-four hours we have blown up and destroyed bridges, tunnels, and private property to the value of £40,000,000 to stop the advance of the cowardly aggressors who sought to make us buy peace at the price of our honour.

"We are doing the duty imposed upon us by international obligations. Will England delay to do hers until Belgium is turned into a gigantic cemetery in which will be buried our dead and her national honour; and while I, through this Chamber, make this supreme appeal to the great British nation and to the whole of the British Empire, Liège and her sister forts are keeping the flag of our national honour flying?

"Now and in view of every eventuality our valiant youth is ready. In the name of the nation I address to them a fraternal salutation. But one duty is theirs—an obstinate resistance.

"The moment is now for deeds."

An indescribable ovation greeted this declaration, which was made in firm and decisive tones. The Socialist leaders joined in the tempests of applause.

After the departure of the King and Queen, the Premier, Baron de Broqueville, made the following statement:—

"By accepting the German demands we would sacrifice the honour of the nation. Germany informed us at six o'clock this morning that she sees herself compelled to carry out military plans even with the use of force.

"We can be conquered, but not crushed and never reduced to submission."

GERMAN TAVERNS SACKED.

From Our Own Correspondent.

ANTWERP, Tuesday, 11.10 p.m.

Patriotic demonstrations are being held all over the town to-night. Manifestations have been made against the larger German-owned shops and hotels, which had to hoist the Belgian flag to appease the crowd. Several small German taverns near the harbour were sacked, and other German establishments are now being guarded by the military.

7.30 a.m. EDITION

30 GERMANS DROWNED.

TORPEDO BOAT SUNK.

FROM OUR SPECIAL CORRESPONDENT.

COPENHAGEN, Tuesday, 11.25 p.m.

A German torpedo-boat to-day suddenly sank at the Gjedser Lighthouse, six miles from Gjedser, off the south Danish coast.

From the lighthouse it was observed that some sailors jumped overboard when the torpedo-boat sank, and a boat was despatched for assistance. It picked up a few sailors.

Thirty officers and men were drowned. The survivors declared that the boiler on board the torpedo-boat exploded.

BOMBS FROM THE AIR.

GERMAN AIRMAN OVER FRENCH FRONTIER TOWN.

From Our Own Correspondent.

PARIS, Monday Night.

A German aeroplane appeared to-day over Lunéville, an important garrison town on the French frontier, and dropped three bombs, causing some damage but no loss of life.

Tuesday, 8.30 p.m.

The Germans have entered the village of Moineville, near Nancy. They have shot the village priest.

PARIS, Tuesday.

A German company is reported to be in French territory near Mars-la-Tour, the scene of one of the most sanguinary battles of the war of 1870.—Reuter.

Mars-la-Tour is a French village fourteen miles south-west of the German fortress of Metz.

GERMAN NAVAL RAID.

MEDITERRANEAN PORTS SHELLED.

From Our Own Correspondent.

PARIS, Tuesday, 3.50 p.m.

It is stated at the Ministry of Foreign Affairs that the German cruiser Breslau has bombarded Bona and Bougie, on the Algerian coast.

After firing sixty shells the warship sailed to the west.

Tuesday, 8.30 p.m.

The Breslau has also bombarded Philippeville, approaching under the Russian flag.

PARIS, Tuesday.

The Governor-General of Algeria reports that at four o'clock this morning a four-funnelled cruiser, thought to be the German cruiser Breslau, discharged eight broadsides at the town of Bona, sixty shells being fired. One man was killed and some houses were damaged.

She then steamed towards the west.—Reuter.

The Breslau is a small cruiser. She was last heard of in the Adriatic. She has twelve 4.1in. guns.

WARSHIP ON THE WATCH.

ST. PETERSBURG, Tuesday.

The following telegram has been received here from Tokio:—

"Yesterday a German warship was observed in the Strait of Tsushima watching the ships of the Russian Volunteer Fleet. The Japanese Fleet is quite ready to put to sea."—Reuter.

Tsushima was the scene of the last naval battle, nine years ago, when the Japanese destroyed the Russian Baltic Fleet.

BURNING VILLAGES.

GERMANS FALLING BACK BEFORE THE RUSSIANS.

ST. PETERSBURG, Tuesday.

The Russian troops have established contact with the enemy along the greater part of the Russo-German frontier. A reconnaissance has been made on the Bialla and Borzymmen front. The German troops have fallen back a day's march, burning the villages over an enormous stretch of country.—Reuter.

ALL-NIGHT SCENES.

DEMONSTRATING CROWDS ROUND THE PALACE.

Shortly after eleven o'clock last night the King and Queen appeared on the balcony of Buckingham Palace, and the enthusiasm of the crowd was tremendous. At 1.30 this morning the Mall was packed with people marching and singing, and there was still a large number at 3 a.m.

All through the evening there had been crowds waiting in the streets for definite tidings of the approaching conflict. Bands of men and women went marching up and down, singing and waving flags. Motors decorated with the French and English flags paraded through the streets, with rolling cheers following them.

Soon after midnight the news of the declaration of war spread, and in Piccadilly-circus there was a scene of the greatest enthusiasm. The tension of the past few days had become intolerable and, terrible though the news might be, it came as a positive relief. The National Anthem and the Marseillaise were sung.

A great roaring cheer of defiance was the answer of a vast crowd in Trafalgar-square to the news. One vast patriotic shout rent the air. Union Jacks were waved, often in company with the tricolour of France, and processions of people marched round the foot of the Nelson column cheering wildly and singing national airs. Hooting motor-cars picked their way through the mass, with people piled on the roof and all the passengers waving Union Jacks. The scene was one of extraordinary and surpassing enthusiasm.

EMPRESS AS NURSE.

From Our Own Correspondent.

COPENHAGEN, Tuesday.

The Russian Ambassador at Berlin, M. Sverbeieff, arrived here to-day with the Grand Duchess Xenia's son-in-law, Prince De Youssoupoff, who had been arrested in Berlin and afterwards released.

Princess Youssoupoff was seriously shocked by the Prince's unexpected arrest, and had to be carried to [illegible] from the train [illegible]

WHERE THE FLEETS WILL MEET.

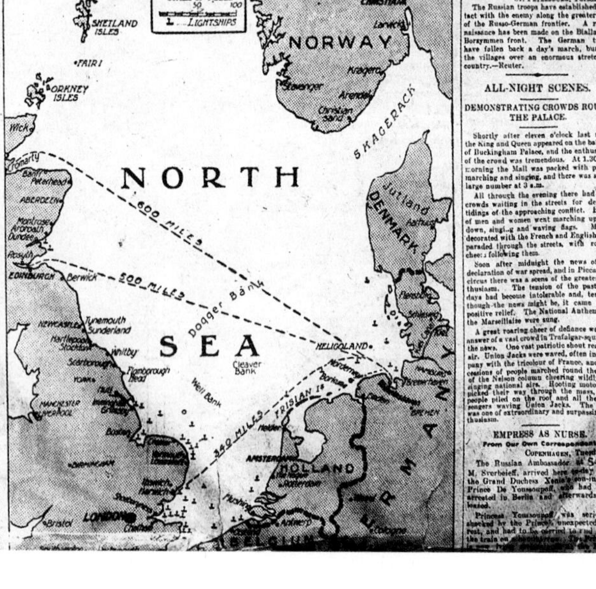

Opposite *The Daily Mail* reports the declaration of war, August 1914. **Below** The Battle of Tannenberg, 26 August 1914. **Bottom** The relentless forward advance of the German army into France in 1914 under the Schlieffen Plan.

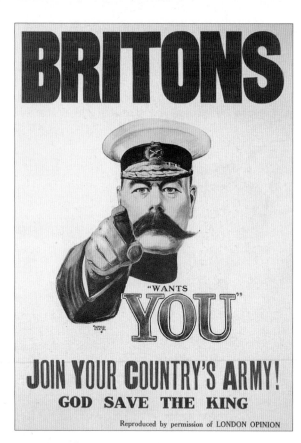

Right This famous Kitchener recruiting poster of 1914 was the most successful of all those produced by the Parliamentary Recruiting Committee. The original drawing by Alfred Leete is in the Imperial War Museum, London. **Below** The response to the recruiting campaigns was overwhelming. This photograph shows recruits enlisting at Southwark Town Hall, London, in 1915.

Above and right Two very effective recruiting posters. Alone among the European belligerents, Britain refused to introduce conscription until 1916, relying instead on volunteers.

Above The first Battle of
Ypres. Men of the 2nd Scots
Guards regiment in a shallow
trench, October 1914. **Right**
The first of the many German
soldiers killed at the Battle of
the Marne, September 1914.
Opposite top On 6 August
1915, three months after the
first landings on the beaches
of the Gallipoli Peninsula, the
Allied commander, Sir Ian
Hamilton, surprised the Turks
by landing a second force
behind their right flank at
Suvla Bay. **Opposite bottom**
A respite from filth, lice and
dysentery – soldiers swim-
ming south of 'X' beach at
Gallipoli.

Below The death-throes of the defeated Serbian army on its retreat through the snows in the mountains of Montenegro, November 1915. **Bottom** French attackers at Verdun caught in the open by German fire.

FIVE

Gallipoli – vision and reality

THE BRITISH HAD ALWAYS INTENDED that the Royal Navy rather than the tiny regular army should be their major contribution to the alliance. The advent of war had shown that the mighty ships that had thrilled British hearts at peacetime Spithead reviews could do little in the short term to influence a land war on the Continent. While the crucial Marne campaign was being decided, the British Grand Fleet, with a superiority of 24 modern battle-ships to the German High Seas Fleet's 16, could only steam impotently about the North Sea. The long-expected 'second Trafalgar' failed to take place. An action in the Heligoland Bight on 28 August 1914 between British battle-cruisers and cruisers and German cruisers, in which four German ships were sunk, made the German command even less inclined to venture far from its home ports. Instead, technology presented new challenges to a maritime supremacy based on the battleship. On 22 September 1914 the submarine U-9 sank three British armoured cruisers, *Hawke*, *Cressy* and *Aboukir* off the Dutch coast, and on 23 October the modern battleship *Audacious* succumbed to a mine off northern Ireland. By 1915 the submarine, once seen merely as a coastal-defence weapon, had emerged as a major threat to Allied commerce. For the first time in history the power enjoying maritime supremacy found itself under increasingly effective blockade.

Instead of a triumphant Trafalgar in the North Sea, the British public had to content itself with news of dramatic but strategically minor actions in the far oceans. On 1 November Admiral Sir Christopher Cradock's obsolete armoured cruiser squadron was destroyed by Admiral Graf von Spee in the Battle of Coronel off the Chilean coast. Stung by this affront to the Nelson tradition, Winston Churchill, the First Lord of the Admiralty, dispatched the battle-cruisers *Invincible* and *Inflexible* to hunt Spee's cruisers down. In the Battle of the Falkland Isles on 8 December the 12-inch armament of the British ships outranged and over-whelmed the enemy, but only after a display of superbly accurate German and disquietingly random British gunnery. Meanwhile, on 9 November, the cruiser HMAS *Sydney* had sunk the German commerce-raiding cruiser *Emden* at the Cocos Islands, a first kill for the young Australian navy.

Yet for all the absence of a great clash between the battle fleets, British seapower had swept enemy commerce from the oceans from the very outbreak of war. Geography itself, placing the British Isles athwart Germany's sea exits to the world, was on Britain's side. Safe under the White Ensign, the BEF crossed to France, and the armies of the British Empire – from Australia,

New Zealand, India and Canada – sailed to join in the Mother Country's struggle. Thanks to the Royal Navy, German industry lay cut off from key raw materials; Britain and France instead of Germany and Austria were able to tap America's vast potential for munitions production – a factor that in literal truth was to be the saving of the Allied cause in 1915–16. Nor, unlike in the Second World War, did Britain have to fear another fleet at the far end of the world, for Japan declared war on Germany on 21 August 1914 in accordance with the Anglo-Japanese alliance, and in pursuit of her own expansionist ambitions.

So the conflict rippled further and further from Europe itself. Japanese and British forces successfully attacked Tsingtau, the German base on the China coast. South African forces invaded German South West Africa. Other imperial forces attacked German East Africa, but with disastrous results, for Paul von Lettow-Vorbeck, the German commander, proved so skilful and resolute that from first to last he drew in a total of at least 130,000 British Empire troops against his 3,500 German and 12,000 African soldiers, and was still in the field when the war ended in 1918.

The Middle East too had become a theatre of war, and partly because of an unfortunate lapse of British seapower. In August 1914 two German battle-cruisers, *Goeben* and *Breslau*, had escaped the Mediterranean Fleet as a result of ambiguous orders and misunderstandings between the Admiralty, the Commander-in-Chief and the admiral on the spot, and taken refuge at Constantinople, the capital of the then neutral Turkish Empire. These two powerful ships proved instrumental in Germany's successful diplomatic efforts to drag Turkey into the war on her side. British, Australian, Indian and New Zealand troops flowed into Egypt to protect the Suez Canal from the Turkish army in Palestine (then part of the Turkish Empire), and more imperial troops landed at Basra at the head of the Persian Gulf to protect the vital Persian oilfields from Turkish troops in Mesopotamia. And far to the north, up in the bleak mountain country of Armenia on the Russo-Turkish border, the Turks launched a ferocious offensive in bitter winter weather against the hard-pressed Russian armies.

In the winter and spring of 1915 both sides sought by bribes and pressure to turn remaining neutrals into allies. Secret Allied offers of Austrian territory down the Dalmatian coast and even of Turkish territory induced Italy to betray her alliance with the central powers and declare war on Austria on 3 May 1915. The roar of guns, the death of men, extended to the mountains that ring the north Italian plain, as the Italians launched the first of the 11 battles of the Isonzo (four of them in 1915), attempting to strike eastwards against Austria between Gorizia and Trieste. But in London especially, this desire to recruit neutrals into the war blended with the purely strategic search for likely operations elsewhere than the Western Front. Winston Churchill favoured the seaborne capture of Borkum in the East Frisian Islands, which he believed could lead to the invasion of northern Germany and probably induce Holland to join the Allies. Others favoured the eastern Mediterranean; Lloyd George wished to send an army to

---

Opposite: **Gallipoli 1915–16.** The hatched area shows the extent of land occupied by the Allied forces.

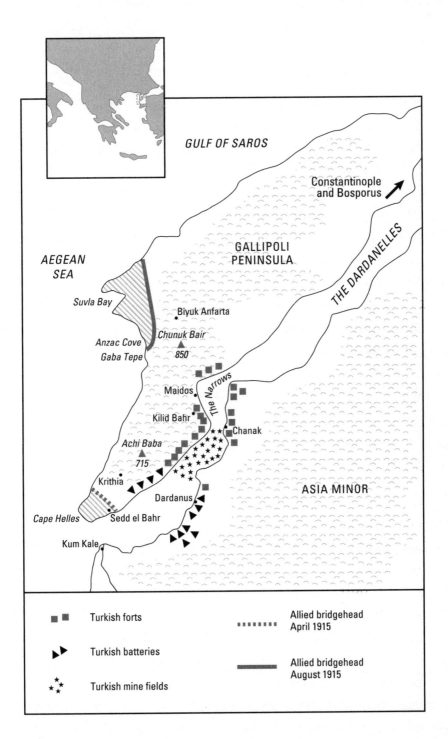

GULF OF SAROS

Constantinople
and Bosporus

GALLIPOLI
PENINSULA

THE DARDANELLES

AEGEAN
SEA

Suvla Bay

Biyuk Anfarta

Anzac Cove

Chunuk Bair
850

Gaba Tepe

The Narrows

Maidos

Kilid Bahr

Chanak

Achi Baba
715

Krithia

ASIA MINOR

Dardanus

Cape Helles

Sedd el Bahr

Kum Kale

■ ■ Turkish forts	▪▪▪▪▪▪▪▪ Allied bridgehead April 1915
▲ ▶ Turkish batteries	▬▬▬▬ Allied bridgehead August 1915
★ ★ Turkish mine fields	

help Serbia; since Serbia was landlocked, the possibility of neutral Greece receiving Allied forces in Salonika was canvassed. Then again, perhaps Greece, Bulgaria and Romania could be induced to fall upon either Austria or Turkey. In January 1915 Russia, hard-pressed in Armenia, pleaded for Allied action against Turkey. Eyes now focused on the Dardanelles, the straits between Asia Minor and the Gallipoli Peninsula leading to the Sea of Marmara and Constantinople. If the Dardanelles could be forced and Constantinople and the Bosporus mastered, the strategic prizes could be enormous. Anatolian Turkey would be severed from Europe; the Turkish heartland and the Turkish armies in Armenia, Mesopotamia and the Sinai Peninsula would be cut off from German war supplies; Turkey might well sue for peace. With Allied forces through the Dardanelles, it seemed possible that Romania, Bulgaria and Greece might join the Allied cause. Enticing visions beckoned of expeditions up the Danube leading to Austria's collapse. To the majority of British leaders at the beginning of 1915 such a Levant and Balkan strategy seemed a splendid way of outflanking on a continental scale the German trench fortress in France. Churchill in particular threw himself into promoting and preparing a purely naval attack on the Dardanelles.

Yet a pre-war staff study had concluded that only a combined sea and land assault could hope to defeat the forts that com-manded the Dardanelles from each shore. Such an amphibious operation demanded well-trained, well-equipped troops with experienced task force headquarters, and all the specialized equipment and communications necessary to put an army on a hostile coast and maintain it there. It required a thoroughly rehearsed assault force with plenty of reserves for the break-out and exploitation. Above all it needed preparation in secrecy and a sudden descent on an unalerted enemy. None of these requirements was satisfied. The tragedy of the Dardanelles campaign was to lie in the mismatching of a daring strategic idea to defective means and muffed opportunities.

As early as 3 November 1914 warships under Churchill's instructions had bombarded for 10 minutes the outer Turkish forts guarding the entrance to the straits. It was enough to set the Turks, under German guidance, to reorganizing their defences and laying mine barriers. On 13 January 1915 the War Council of the British Cabinet approved Churchill's proposals for a purely naval attempt to force the Dardanelles by silencing the forts by gunfire and sweeping the minefields – proposals that Admiral Sir John Fisher, the First Sea Lord, and other naval experts reckoned impracticable, believing that the attack must be a combined operation. On 19 February the navy began a systematic attempt to demolish the forts as a preliminary to sweeping the mines. However, to demolish such forts heavy howitzers were needed, like those employed by the Germans against Liège, rather than flat-trajectory naval guns. By 11 March the step-by-step Allied bombardment had silenced only the outer forts; the inner ones covering the minefields remained intact. Meanwhile, the Turks were steadily strengthening their own forces. As Fisher wrote, 'Things are going badly at the Dardanelles! We want military cooperation, as pointed out by me in January... Now we are held up for want of soldiers!'

The disposable strategic reserve of the British Empire at this time consisted of one regular division, the 29th. Should it go to France – or the Mediterranean? Reluctantly Kitchener released it for the Mediterranean. Unfortunately its transports were not combat-loaded, so they had first to be sent to Egypt to be emptied and repacked. The army could not be ready to land on Gallipoli and open the way for the navy until the third week of April. At Churchill's behest, the Allied fleet, instead of waiting, attempted to rush the straits in one grand attack on 18 March. The attempt failed at the cost of three battleships sunk by mines and three further ships disabled.

Although there was now rising doubt in London about going on with operations against the Dardanelles, Churchill and Kitchener carried the day. On 25 April, six months after the first bombardment of the Dardanelles forts, the Allied expeditionary force under General Sir Ian Hamilton landed on the beaches of the Gallipoli Peninsula.

The Turks were commanded by an able German general, Otto Liman von Sanders; they fought with dogged courage and a remarkable indifference to casualties. On the British side everything that can go wrong with under-rehearsed amphibious operations lacking all kinds of specialized equipment (and, perhaps most of all, an experienced combined headquarters) went wrong. The fighting was savage, bloody, muddled. The Western Front lesson, that human bodies in the open were no match for artillery and machine guns, was repeated on the steep, rocky slopes that led from the narrow beaches. The expeditionary force found itself penned into two narrow lodgements – the British and French around Cape Helles, at the tip of the Gallipoli Peninsula, and the Anzac Corps (Australian and New Zealand Army Corps) at 'Anzac Cove' on the western coast. Instead of the swift capture of the Peninsula, opening the way for the navy to sail on to Constantinople, there ensued stalemate and trench warfare perhaps even more ghastly than the Western Front, in which the stench of corpses rotting in the blazing sun of May, June and July blended with the perfume of wild thyme, and the very narrowness of the front and the rear areas added a dreadful claustrophobia. Attack, counter-attack, further attack followed one on another across the rocky ground, fighting for possession of some ridge or height in Gallipoli's steep and complex terrain. The stoicism of the British, the élan of the French, the high-spirited verve of the Anzacs found their match in the unyielding stubbornness of the Turk. On 24 May a 'suspension of arms' took place so that both sides might bury the dead. 'Everywhere Turks were digging and digging graves for some 4,000 of their countrymen who had been putrefying in heaps along their narrow front for nearly a month in the warm May air,' wrote Compton Mackenzie. A soldier said to him: 'You've got your foot in an awkward place.' He looked down and saw 'squelching up from the ground on either side of my boot like a rotten mangold the deliquescent green and black flesh of a Turk's head'.

On 6 August the Allied commander, Sir Ian Hamilton, attempted to regain the initiative by landing a fresh force at Suvla, behind the Turkish right flank. The Turks were taken by surprise; by sunset the attackers outnumbered the immediate defenders by 15 to one; a decisive victory waited to be seized. But Sir Frederick

Stopford, the British commander at Suvla, was old and slow; the New Army divisions employed were raw formations fresh from the voyage from England; the beach-head area lay in utter confusion. Instead of thrusting inland, Stopford's force sat down where it was; the Turks sealed off the new landing; and the stalemate continued – on a wider front.

Gallipoli now became a hell for the combatants, a hell of the spirit because of failure, disappointment and disillusion, and a hell to the body because of the squalor and disease. In September 78 per cent of the Anzacs in seven battalions examined were suffering from dysentery, and 60 per cent from skin sores. The medical care, even at the base hospitals on the island of Lemnos and in Egypt, bore comparison with the Crimea rather than with the standards now being set in British army hospitals in Flanders: another consequence of the hasty improvisation that bedevilled every aspect of the Gallipoli campaign from the very start. Even the spirit of the Anzacs sagged.

A. P. Herbert wrote:

The flies! oh God, the flies
That soiled the sacred dead.
To see them swarm from dead men's eyes
And share the soldiers' bread!
Nor think I now forget
The filth and stench of war,
The corpses on the parapet,
The maggots in the floor.

With autumn came mounting criticism of Hamilton's leadership, both within the expeditionary force and in London. The opponents of the whole Dardanelles strategy, such as Bonar Law, Lloyd George and Lord Milner, urged evacuation. Churchill, now demoted to Chancellor of the Duchy of Lancaster, argued tenaciously for yet further efforts at breaking through. On 6 October Hamilton, too much of a gentleman and too little of a hard-minded, hard-willed commander, was replaced by General Sir Charles Monro, who was quite the opposite. On 21 October Monro reported to London:

> The troops on the Peninsula – with the exception of the Australian and New Zealand Corps – are not equal to a sustained effort owing to the inexperience of the officers, the want of training of the men, and the depleted condition of many of the units... I am therefore of the opinion that another attempt to carry the Turkish lines would not offer any hope of success. On purely military grounds I recommend the evacuation of the Peninsula.

While the government havered, the troops endured. In November Gallipoli produced an unexpected horror: frostbite for 15,000 men. On the 22nd, Kitchener, after visiting the Peninsula himself, advised the Cabinet that Gallipoli should be evacuated. In any event, larger political and strategic developments were dooming the enterprise. In September Bulgaria finally chose to enter the war on the German side, leading both Serbia and Greece to request Allied military support. Greece henceforward took priority over Gallipoli. At the end of November the Cabinet decided on evacuation, whereupon Churchill resigned, his career at its lowest point.

It was feared that up to 40,000 men might be lost in the course of evacuation, but in the event, excellent staff work and elaborate measures of deception enabled General Sir William Birdwood (now the force commander) to bring the troops off without loss. Suvla Bay and Anzac Cove were evacuated on 19 December 1915, and Cape Helles on 18 January 1916.

In all 410,000 British Empire troops and 79,000 French had served on Gallipoli. The total of killed, wounded and missing, dead from disease and evacuated sick was 205,000 British Empire and 47,000 French. The Turks lost some 250,000. Nothing had been achieved. Was the plan to force the Dardanelles and sail to Constantinople – brilliant as an idea – ever a realistic practical proposition? The controversy still goes on. Supporters of the Dardanelles strategy point to the 'might have beens', those brief opportunities when bold and well-organized thrusts could have exploited moments of Turkish weakness. Yet so many missed 'might have beens' really confirm a basic truth: that everything about the expedition was too improvised, too unrehearsed, for it to have the chance of success enjoyed by the thoroughly prepared and equipped Allied amphibious operations in the Second World War.

Yet for Australia and New Zealand Gallipoli served as a furnace that forged a new pride of nationhood. The memory of the grim fights for such localities as 'Lone Pine' and 'Bloody Angle', and of the men who died there, was to be cherished and celebrated down the years; the survivors, the returned servicemen, were not forgotten or neglected, but became a powerful element in the national life.

Gallipoli did not, however, complete the tally of Allied disasters in 1915. In November little Serbia's turn came again, and this time there were Germans to stiffen the Austrians; Bulgarians to take the Serbian army in the rear.

SIX

France will bleed to death

ON 5 OCTOBER 1915 French troops began disembarking at the neutral Greek port of Salonika, vanguard of an Anglo-French expedition intended to bring succour to landlocked Serbia only 50 miles distant along a double-tracked railway. The Allied troops were arriving in response to an appeal by the pro-Allied Greek premier Eleutherios Venizelos, to whom the Serbs had already appealed for help under a treaty of alliance that bound Greece and Serbia to go to each other's aid if either were attacked by Bulgaria. Serbia had learned that Bulgaria, under its German-born king, 'Foxy Ferdinand', had finally decided to join the central powers, Germany and Austria in a combined offensive against her.

As if all this were not Balkan intrigue enough, Venizelos was dismissed from office on the very day Allied troops began to set foot on Greek soil, for the Greek king, Constantine, was himself pro-German, being married to the Kaiser's sister. He was not, however, so pro-German that he wanted to bring down on his country the full rigours of Allied hostility, such as a blockade. He therefore cunningly accepted the Allied presence in Greece, but under protest, so preserving a neutral stance. The Allied forces continued to build up in a strange strategic limbo, their further employment dependent on Greek good will.

On 7 October the long-prepared Austro-German offensives smashed across the rivers Save and Danube into northern Serbia. Two days later the capital, Belgrade, fell. Commanded by the formidable Mackensen, victor of Gorlice-Tarnów, the Austro-German forces drove the outnumbered Serbs into the mountainous heart of the country. Meanwhile, the Bulgarians, striking westwards, had blocked the Vardar valley, the only route by which the Allied forces at Salonika could link up with the Serbs. Although the French advanced to the rescue with covert Greek permission, they arrived too late and in too small numbers. Repelled by Bulgarian forces, they fell back across the Greek frontier, and Serbia was left to die alone. In mid-November the first snows fell in the mountains; the retreat of the Serbian army, encumbered by thousands of refugees, old men, women and children, became one of the most tragic and terrible episodes of the whole war. Before the final struggle over the mountains of Montenegro to the waiting Allied ships on the Adriatic coast, the refugees had to be abandoned to Bulgarian mercy and to the swifter fates of starvation, cold, typhus and dysentery. Only 100,000 men, a quarter of the Serbian army's original strength, reached safety. Eighteen months of gallant but ultimately unavailing resistance had cost Serbia one-sixth of her entire population. So at last, thanks to

German and Bulgarian aid, Austria exacted her full revenge for the Archduke Franz Ferdinand's assassination at Sarajevo.

'The year 1915,' wrote General Joffre, 'was dragging to a close under conditions that brought small comfort to the Allies. Our armies had everywhere been checked or beaten – the enemy appeared to have succeeded in all his undertakings.'

•

NEVERTHELESS, with the military balance so heavily tilted in favour of the central powers, it occurred to no Allied government to think of seeking peace on what could only be enemy terms. Instead the Allies looked forward to redressing the balance in 1916, when, for the first time, the British army would enter the struggle en masse and Allied and American munitions would at last begin to reach the fronts in abundance. In November and December 1915 two inter-Allied military conferences at Joffre's headquarters at Chantilly decided broad Allied strategy for 1916. The sideshows in the Mediterranean and Middle East were to be kept going with merely minimum forces, the Allied representatives being 'unanimous in recognizing that the decision of the war can only be obtained in the principal theatres' – that is, the Russian Front, the Western Front and the Italian Front. 'Decisive results,' the Allies agreed, 'will only be obtained if the offensives of the Armies of the Coalition are made simultaneously, or at least at dates so near together that the enemy will not be able to transport reserves from one front to another.' This concentric squeeze on the central powers was to take place as soon as possible after March. Unfortunately, on 21 February 1916 Germany struck first.

Erich von Falkenhayn, the German Chief of Staff, a prudent, clear-minded soldier, did not propose to embark on some gigantic military gamble aimed at winning the war outright. Rather he wished to compel the Allies to make peace by crippling them militarily and destroying their will to go on. He believed he had already succeeded with Russia in his 1915 offensive; now he meant to do the same in the west. In a memorandum to the Kaiser in December 1915 he argued that Germany could best strike at her arch-enemy England by crippling France:

> ...If we succeeded in opening the eyes of her [France's] people to the fact that in a military sense they have nothing more to hope for, that breaking point would be reached and England's best sword would be knocked out of her hand. To achieve that object the uncertain method of a mass breakthrough, in any case beyond our means, is unnecessary. We can probably do enough for our purposes with limited resources. Within our reach behind the French sector of the Western Front there are objectives for the retention of which the French General Staff would be compelled to throw in every man they have. If they do so, the forces of France will bleed to death – as there can be no question of a voluntary withdrawal – whether we reach our goal or not.

As the objective for which the French would bleed themselves to death, Falkenhayn chose the fortress of Verdun on the Meuse – a place of legendary significance in French history, and the linchpin of the French line during the Marne campaign. He assembled over 1,220 guns on a front of only eight miles, with no fewer than 542 heavy weapons on the main sector of assault – a gigantic mincing machine into which the French army would feed itself to destruction. The role of the German infantry was to be merely subsidiary: to advance just sufficiently to force the enemy into the maw of the mincer. Here was a new military concept: no longer the traditional aims of victory through offensive manoeuvre, through breakthroughs and outflanking thrusts, but war as pure technology; industrialized killing. As January turned to February, the last of the guns were being slotted into positions under their camouflage nets, the last of the assault troops disappearing into their concrete shelters or *Stollen* behind the front line. By 11 February, eve of the attack, all had been done that German thoroughness could do to render Operation *Gericht* (Judgement) a success.

The French defences on the Verdun sector ought to have been among the strongest in the entire Allied line. A girdle of steeply tumbled hills, thick with woods, covered the city from the north: superb defensive country. Ingeniously sited to command the slopes and narrow valleys of this terrain lay some 20 large, pre-war reinforced-concrete forts and 40 smaller ones with interlocking zones of fire. In fact complacency, neglect and mistaken decisions had instead rendered Verdun one of the most vulnerable of sectors. Since 1914 the French high command had largely stripped the forts of their armament, especially the heavy 155-millimetre guns, partly because after the fate of the Belgian fortress of Liège they had come to believe that forts could not withstand modern artillery, partly because they desperately needed heavy guns to support their own field operations. Moreover, the Verdun sector had been tranquil for so long that the French had starved it of reinforcements and had neglected to complete an adequate trench system. In vain had General Frédéric Herr, the fortress commander, warned the high command of Verdun's weaknesses and deficiencies. Fortunately for France, however, Emile Driant, a member of the Chamber of Deputies with a reputation as an expert on military affairs, was serving at Verdun as a lieutenant-colonel. He bypassed the whole chain of command by reporting direct to his fellow parliamentarians in Paris. As a result, the Minister of War prodded Joffre; Joffre sent his deputy, General Edouard de Castelnau, to Verdun to report; Joffre himself followed; then President Poincaré. Very belatedly, in the last week of January, the French began to improve Verdun's defences and reinforce its garrison.

On 12 February, when the German bombardment was due to start, a blizzard blinded the guns and their spotting aircraft and balloons, forcing a week's postponement and giving the French a vital respite. Even so, the odds remained heavily in German favour – over 850 guns on the main front of attack on the right bank of the Meuse against 270; 72 battalions of superbly trained infantry against 34 in still uncompleted trenches. At dawn on 21 February 1916 Falkenhayn's giant mincing machine began its work.

No such concentrated bombardment had ever before been seen in war. The equivalent of up to 2,400 heavy shells fell on each area of ground the size of a football pitch, slicing and chewing and ripping the French defences, defenders and communications to shreds. At 4 p.m. German fighting patrols probed forward into the wilderness to reconnoitre the advance of the assault troops; they carried a new gift of technology to warfare, the flame-thrower, to hose French survivors from their hiding places with liquid fire. Next day the German infantry fell upon the stunned defence, which swiftly crumbled despite the heroism of handfuls of French soldiers fighting on in shellholes and fragments of trench. By the fourth day of Operation *Gericht* the Germans were through the French first and second trench lines and into open country. Only the partially disarmed and lightly garrisoned pre-war forts themselves now stood between the attackers and Verdun. On 25 February the most powerful of all the Verdun forts, Douaumont, with a garrison of only 56 elderly reservists, fell to a small storming party of Brandenburgers. The German army had now achieved just as successful an initial breakthrough on the Western Front as it had at Gorlice-Tarnów on the Eastern the previous year. Yet, by an irony, this had not been Falkenhayn's object at all. If he had now had ready a mass of divisions to swarm through the gap, he might well have brought about a general collapse of the French Front similar to the Russian collapse in 1915. Instead, however, there was only the modest assault force of nine divisions designed for his limited 'mincing' operation, and its advance was slow and deliberate rather than thrusting.

Nevertheless, it seemed to the French that they faced imminent catastrophe. All remaining civilians were evacuated from the city of Verdun itself and the bridges over the Meuse prepared for demolition. Should Verdun be given up? It was Joffre's Chief of Staff, de Castelnau, who, visiting the stricken front, decided that

Verdun could and should be held. So France took Falkenhayn's bait after all. General Philippe Pétain, commander of the Second Army, a realist among generals who believed more in firepower than élan, was appointed to command the defence. The immediate German advance was held, thanks to the gallantry of small pockets of resistance and the German failure to drive on fast in the wake of the bombardment. Now the real mincing began – week after week of it. Pétain believed in rotating units so that each spent only a short time in the hell of noise and lethal metal that was the battlefield of Verdun. By the beginning of May, 40 French divisions were to march in turn up the single narrow road in the salient that led to the fortress – the *Voie Sacrée* (Sacred Way) in French memory. Pétain, rare among generals of his time for his sensitive awareness of his soldiers' sufferings, watched them pass his headquarters at Souilly:

> My heart lurched as I saw our young men of twenty going into the furnace of Verdun, and reflected that they would pass too quickly from the enthusiasm of their first engagement to the weariness caused by suffering…how saddening it was when they came back, either on their own as wounded or stragglers, or in the ranks of companies decimated by loss! Their stares seemed to be fixed in a vision of unbelievable terror…they drooped beneath the weight of their horrifying memories. When I spoke to them, they could scarcely answer.

An average of 1,700 motor trucks a day rolled on their solid tyres along the *Voie Sacrée's* crumbling, constantly repaired surface to nourish the battle; a triumph of organization and effort; the first time in history that the issue of a great battle depended entirely on motor transport. As Pétain, the believer in firepower, built up the strength of the French artillery, German casualty rates began to approach those of the French. The attackers too were being fed through the mincer. As early as the beginning of March it was Falkenhayn's turn to make a decision. Verdun had now become a symbol to the Germans as well as the French, the more so because the offensive lay under the immediate command of the Imperial Crown Prince, 'Little Willy'. Caught by his own psychological stratagem, Falkenhayn decided to widen the front of attack to the left, or west, bank of the Meuse. On 6 March the new offensive opened in another hammer blow of high explosive. Again there were initial successes against a stunned and shredded defence; again, however, the French were able to cordon off the attackers. The familiar pattern resumed of attack and counter-attack under an endless hail of shell, as the Germans strove to push the French off the commanding heights of Côte 304 and the sinisterly named *Le Mort Homme* (The Dead Man).

By the end of March German casualties at Verdun had reached 81,607; the French 89,000. The mincer ground on – through April, through May, through June. Here was another appalling novelty, for even the vain French offensives of 1915 had lasted only a few weeks each. Churned and rechurned by shellfire, the battlefield attained a horror without precedent in war. To an airman high above, it resembled the 'humid skin of a monstrous toad'. The infantryman on the ground 'found the dead embedded in the walls of the trenches, heads, legs and half-bodies', or saw comrades 'laid open from the shoulders to the haunches like a carcass of meat in a butcher's window'. The whole battlefield was now an open cemetery, constantly turned over by the guns, stinking in the spring sunshine. 'You ate beside the dead,' wrote a French soldier. 'You drank beside the dead. You relieved yourself beside the dead. You slept beside the dead.' And still Falkenhayn's mincer worked on.

•

ON 26 MAY JOFFRE visited Sir Douglas Haig, the British Commander-in-Chief, in order to confer about the date for the long-projected Anglo-French offensive astride the River Somme. 'The moment I mentioned August 15th,' wrote Haig in his diary, 'Joffre at once got very excited and shouted that "the French army would cease to exist then if we did nothing till then".' Yet Haig was deeply and legitimately concerned about the rawness of his own army and the consequences of committing it prematurely to an offensive against the immensely strong German defences on the Somme. As he wrote in March: 'I have not an army in France really, but a collection of divisions untrained for the field.' Nevertheless he recognized that the British army could not long remain idle while the French bled to death at Verdun; by now French casualties there had passed 200,000. He promised Joffre that the British offensive would open on 1 July.

On 8 June the Germans launched a fresh offensive at Verdun on the east bank of the Meuse. Fort Vaux fell after a heroic defence by Commandant Raynal in a nightmare fight in the fort's underground passages. There were ominous signs that French morale in general was beginning to crumble at last. The German advance got to within two-and-a-half miles of the city, and Pétain, now promoted to Army Group Commander, contemplated evacuating the whole east bank sector. Even Joffre grew uneasy. By 12 June the new sector commander at Verdun, General Robert Nivelle, had only a single fresh brigade in reserve. Then, on the verge of final success, the German onslaught faltered. For this the French had to thank their Russian ally. On 4 June General Aleksei Brusilov struck the Austrian Front in Galicia with 50 divisions. The Austrians stampeded in total rout, ultimately losing 400,000 in prisoners alone. On 8 June Conrad von Hötzendorf, the Austrian Chief of Staff, appealed to Falkenhayn for help; Falkenhayn dispatched three divisions from the west and called a temporary halt at Verdun. On 23 June, against the urging of the Imperial Crown Prince, the local army commander, he ordered the attack to be resumed. But he had missed his moment, for Nivelle had had time to rebuild his reserves and his defences. On 24 June the British guns opened their preliminary bombardment on the Somme.

SEVEN

The Battle of the Somme

AT 7.30 A.M. ON 1 JULY 1916, 14 British divisions climbed out of their trenches along an 18-mile front north of the Somme and marched slowly forward, each man carrying 66 pounds of kit, in wave after wave of extended lines, steadily on towards the German defences. They expected to find the enemy barbed wire, trench systems, artillery and defenders all annihilated by the week-long preliminary bombardment by 1,350 guns. Instead they were massacred by German artillery and machine guns, first as they plodded across no-man's-land and then as they bunched to struggle through such gaps as existed in the often uncut barbed wire. By the end of the day no fewer than 57,000 men had fallen, 19,000 of them killed, and without gaining a lodgement in the German defences, except on the right of the line next to the five French divisions also taking part in the offensive.

A catastrophe without parallel in British history, this first day on the Somme still continues to provoke ferocious indictments of Sir Douglas Haig and his subordinates. Undoubtedly they committed errors of judgement tragic in their consequences, even if the errors are more easily perceived with hindsight. But the causes of the catastrophe are to be found as much in iron circumstance as in the mistakes of the British high command.

The location of the Allied offensive for 1916 on the sector astride the Somme, opposite an immensely strong part of the German line, was chosen by Joffre, for little better strategic reason than that this was the junction point between the French and British armies. Since France was still the senior military partner in the alliance, Haig deferred to Joffre's wishes, even though he would have preferred to attack in Flanders, where the German defences were as yet not so elaborate. It was Joffre's urgent appeals to Haig to relieve the German pressure on Verdun that also determined the premature launching of the offensive, six weeks before Haig himself thought his green formations could be ready for battle.

Green they were: a necessary consequence of Britain, unlike other belligerents, having to create a mass army from scratch after the outbreak of war and, a further handicap, deploy it and maintain it across the sea. The task had been accomplished in less than two years; an astounding achievement. The original BEF of four infantry divisions and one of cavalry had grown by July 1916 into 58 divisions organized in four armies, soon to be five. The number of heavy artillery batteries was five times greater than at the beginning of 1915, while the number of squadrons in the Royal Flying Corps had more than doubled in a year. The administrative feat of installing and supplying a force of nearly one and half million men in the bare downlands of Picardy and the plains of Flanders was itself gigantic. A mass of soldiers as numerous as the population of a great city had to be given shelter, water supplies, sanitation, medical services, daily hot food, clothing, workshops, building and construction services, off-duty entertainment and recreation, a transport network and a telephone system of immense complication. All this had been done with complete success, even though the British army, in peacetime merely a small imperial garrison force, began with nothing like the resources in equipment and trained specialists enjoyed by mass European armies.

On 27 January 1916, with the army in France below establishment, Britain had finally introduced conscription; in May it was extended to married men as well as single. Here was another radical change in British life forced by the demands of total war. Although over a million men had volunteered before the end of 1914, the rate of enlistment fell off steadily during 1915, despite vigorous propaganda campaigns conducted by leading public figures, and despite the white feathers handed by women to men of military age in civilian clothes. By the summer of 1916 the 'New Army' or 'Kitchener's Army' recruits who had begun to learn drill with broomsticks in 1914–15 felt themselves to be fully fledged soldiers; many had taken their turn in quiet sectors of the line. Their spirit and self-confidence were high. Yet compared with the German army, with its abundant, highly trained professional officers and non-commissioned officers, Haig's army was really little better than a militia. At every level, from divisional commanders down to subalterns, there were officers recently promoted to new responsibilities. The staffs of formation headquarters, crammed on wartime short courses, could not compare with their German opposite numbers. By July 1916 even 'regular' fighting units rarely equalled the standard of the old BEF destroyed in the battles of 1914. One commander of a regular battalion confided to his diary on 4 June that his soldiers 'are still not PROPERLY TRAINED, although full of courage.'

This lack of training and experience led to the tactics adopted on the first day of the Battle of the Somme. Haig, a cavalryman himself, suggested an advance in small groups making use of ground in the German or French style. The commander of the Fourth Army, Sir Henry Rawlinson (an infantryman) and his staff believed such flexible tactics to be beyond their troops; they believed that only a deliberate advance in rigid lines could work without confusion. Haig deferred to Rawlinson, as the infantry specialist and the commander responsible for actually conducting the offensive. It was Haig who decided that in order to avoid the delays in exploiting initial success experienced in earlier battles, the reserves should go forward from the support trenches at the

---

Opposite: **Trench Warfare on the Western Front**. Diagrammatic map of the attack by the British 56th Division on the Gommecourt sector on the first day of the Battle of the Somme, 1 July 1916. On the left are the British communication trenches through which the attacking troops reached the front line. On the right is the German defence system, a maze of trenches (shown here with contemporary British code-names) with dug-outs to shelter the garrison from the British bombardment. The plan was to capture the German salient by a pincer movement by 56th Division south of Gommecourt and 46th Division (not shown here) north of the village. Flanking artillery and machine-gun fire cut the attackers down as they crossed no-man's-land. Although 46th Division reached the second German trench (but still far short of the planned first objective shown on this map), enemy counter-attacks forced both divisions out of their temporary gains by late afternoon.

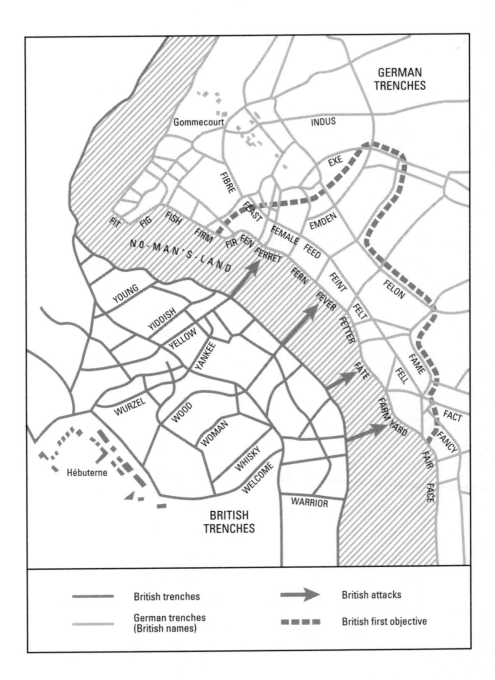

GERMAN
TRENCHES

Gommecourt

INDUS

EXE

FIBRE

FEAST

EMDEN

FIT FIG FISH FIRM

FEMALE FEED

NO-MAN'S-LAND

FIR FEN FERRET

FERN

FEINT

FELON

YOUNG

FEVER

FELT

YIDDISH

FETTER

YELLOW

YANKEE

FATE

FAME

FELL

WURZEL

WOOD

FARMYARD

FACT

WOMAN

FANCY

WHISKY

FAIR

WELCOME

FACE

Hébuterne

WARRIOR

BRITISH
TRENCHES

| | British trenches | | British attacks |
| | German trenches (British names) | | British first objective |

same time as the assault troops advanced from the front line. By keeping the momentum going he hoped to break clean through all three German positions. These tactical decisions combined together to present the Germans with the magnificent target of a deep zone of slowly advancing troops.

However, Haig and Rawlinson had been convinced by their artillery experts that the week-long preliminary bombardment would obliterate the enemy defence as effectively as the German bombardment at Verdun. They therefore saw the infantry advance as more in the nature of an occupation than an assault. The event proved their faith in the preliminary bombardment to be tragically misplaced. For however abundant the guns and shells might seem to gunners who remembered the scarcity of 1915, the weight of fire in proportion to front was well below German or even French standards – some 1,350 guns to 18 miles of front compared to 1,220 German to barely eight miles at Verdun in February. Whereas the German artillery there had included nearly 550 modern heavy pieces and another 150 heavy trench mortars, there were fewer than 400 British heavies on the Somme, and some of them obsolete. Although the War Office had placed the orders for guns and shells back in 1914–15, British and North American industry had failed to live up to its promises of delivery. Moreover, the ammunition produced by firms new to the work often proved defective, and the advancing troops found the ground littered with 'duds'. Unlike the French defences at Verdun in February, the German trench system on the Somme was as strong as time and ingenuity could devise, with shell-proof deep shelters for the infantry.

Such was the anatomy of the disaster of 1 July 1916. It took time for the dimensions of the Fourth Army's failure to reach Haig across the gulf of smashed telephone lines and dead runners. Even then there could be no question of abandoning the offensive, for the first day on the Somme was the 132nd day of the Battle of Verdun. On 2 July Haig wrote: 'The enemy has undoubtedly been severely shaken and he has few reserves in hand. Our correct course, therefore, is to press him hard with the least possible delay. In any case, pressure must be maintained both to relieve Verdun and assist the French on our right.' On the morrow General Fritz von Below, commanding the German Second Army defending the Somme front, issued an order of the day:

> ...We must win this battle in spite of the enemy's temporary superiority in artillery and infantry. The important ground lost in certain places will be recaptured by our attack after the arrival of reinforcements. For the present the important thing is to hold on to our present positions at any cost and improve them by local counter-attack.
>
> I forbid the voluntary evacuation of trenches. The will to stand firm must be impressed on every man in the army. I hold commanding officers responsible for this. The enemy should have to carve his way over heaps of corpses...

In this collision of two stubborn wills and two brave armies was set the pattern of the 140-day Battle of the Somme. Virtually every Allied attack was to be followed by a German counter-attack. The infantry of both sides were to be crushed in turn beneath the anonymous hammer of the guns; to share equally in the terror and the suffering.

Until the end of July Haig believed he might yet achieve his original aim of breaking through the German defences south of Bapaume and, with the cavalry corps in the van, swinging north-wards to bring about a general collapse of the whole German Front between Arras and the Somme. On 14 July, in a remarkable demon-stration of how quickly the British could adapt their methods, four divisions launched a dawn attack after a night assembly in no-man's-land and captured the German second line on a three-mile front. For a fleeting moment it seemed that the way was clear for the cavalry to go through, and one Indian cavalry brigade actually came into action. But the enemy defence quickly thickened again. The familiar Western Front pattern resumed. The names of obscure patches of French woodland, fought over thicket by thicket and glade by glade until nothing remained but splintered stumps amid the corpses and shellholes, became seared into the memory of a generation – Delville Wood, Trones Wood, High Wood. Nevertheless Haig's offensive had already achieved one major objec-tive, for on 11 July Falkenhayn finally closed down his Verdun offensive in order to free reserves for the Somme. Yet the Battle of Verdun still went on, this time with the French on the attack.

On 20 July it was the turn of the Australians to make their debut on the Somme, assaulting northeastwards towards the ruins of Pozières, a village on the crest of the downland between Albert and Bapaume: 'the heaviest, bloodiest, rottenest stunt that ever the Australians were caught up in', according to one Australian recollection. The Australian soldiers reflected Australia's free and

Below German dead behind a machine gun post near Guillemont. **Bottom** A Mark I tank going into battle on the Somme in September 1916 to capture Flers and Courcelette. The soldiers' leather helmets were later discontinued because of their resemblance to German helmets.

Opposite top 'Zero Hour' by James Prinsep Beadle. **Opposite bottom** Packhorses taking ammunition to the front. **Below** A shell-filling factory. At home there was a great industrial expansion for munitions production.

Below German troops outside shelters and dug-outs along the Western Front, 1916.

Below War leadership. Albert Thomas, the French Minister of Armaments (left) and Joseph Joffre, Commander-in-Chief of the French army, look on while Douglas Haig, Commander-in-Chief of the British Expeditionary Force, expounds to British Prime Minister, David Lloyd George (right). **Opposite top** Queues outside food shops in Petrograd in 1917 eventually erupted into a riot which became a revolution. **Opposite bottom** A Russian soldier arresting two deserters. In fact, most Russians yearned for peace on any terms.

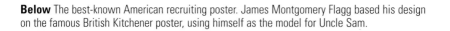
Below The best-known American recruiting poster. James Montgomery Flagg based his design on the famous British Kitchener poster, using himself as the model for Uncle Sam.

easy, egalitarian society, sometimes to the disquiet of British commanders, used to British army discipline and the hierarchical deference to one's 'betters' found in British society. Their aggressiveness and high spirit were unsurpassed. Pozières fell to them on 23 July and its windmill, just beyond, on 5 August. The remains of the mill can still be seen there today, a low grassy mound beside the road, left as a memorial to Australian courage.

In August the Battle of the Somme entered a grimmer phase, for Haig gave up hope of an early breakthrough and resorted to Falkenhayn-like mincing tactics. Germany now lay under a fearful strain, her army remorselessly gripped on the Somme and at Verdun, her Austrian ally falling back before the Russians in Galicia and the Italians north of Trieste. On 27 August Romania entered the war on the Allied side, so adding to the strain. Next day the Kaiser sought an answer to Germany's deepening plight by replacing Falkenhayn with that victorious team Hindenburg and Ludendorff. For the first time since 1914 the German leadership contemplated retreating on the Western Front, for as Ludendorff wrote later, they 'had to face the danger that "Somme fighting" would soon break out at various points on our fronts, and that even our troops would not be able to withstand such attacks indefinitely… Accordingly, the construction had been begun as early as September of powerful rear positions in the West.'

The Allies were therefore not unjustified in thinking that continued offensives on all fronts might make the enemy crack, and so bring peace in 1916. Haig decided that the British contribution to this climactic effort should be a renewed attempt finally to break through on the Somme. This time British inventiveness had

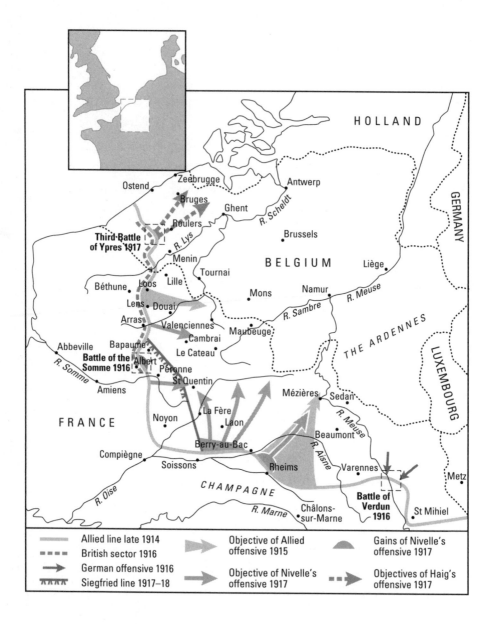

Above: **The Western Front 1914–17.** Opposite (areas marked on the map above): **The Battle of Verdun 1916, the Battle of the Somme 1916 and the Third Battle of Ypres 1917.**

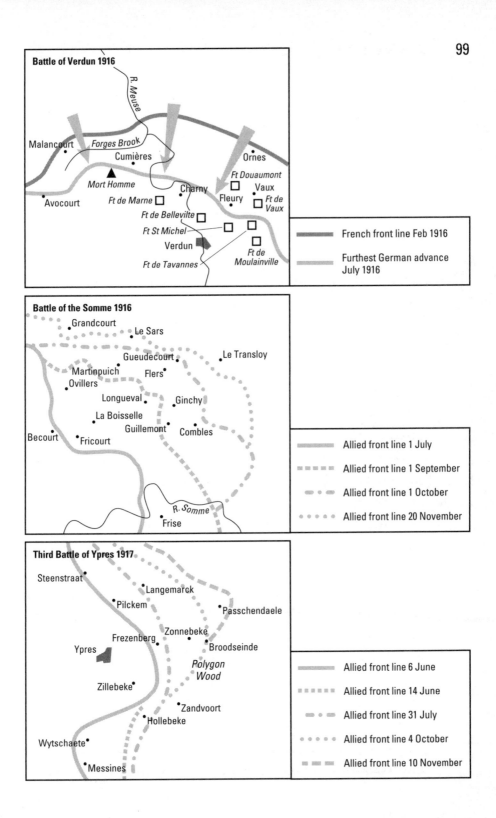

Battle of Verdun 1916

Malancourt
Forges Brook
Cumières
Ornes
Ft Douaumont
Avocourt
Mort Homme
Ft de Marne
Charny
Vaux
Fleury
Ft de Vaux
Ft de Belleville
Ft St Michel
Verdun
Ft de Tavannes
Ft de Moulainville
R. Meuse

▬▬	French front line Feb 1916
▬▬	Furthest German advance July 1916

Battle of the Somme 1916

Grandcourt
Le Sars
Gueudecourt
Le Transloy
Martinpuich
Flers
Ovillers
Longueval
Ginchy
La Boisselle
Guillemont
Combles
Becourt
Fricourt
R. Somme
Frise

	Allied front line 1 July
	Allied front line 1 September
	Allied front line 1 October
	Allied front line 20 November

Third Battle of Ypres 1917

Steenstraat
Langemarck
Pilckem
Passchendaele
Frezenberg
Zonnebeke
Ypres
Broodseinde
Polygon Wood
Zillebeke
Zandvoort
Hollebeke
Wytschaete
Messines

	Allied front line 6 June
	Allied front line 14 June
	Allied front line 31 July
	Allied front line 4 October
	Allied front line 10 November

provided him with a revolutionary new instrument for smashing a path through the enemy wire and trenches – the tank.

The idea of armoured landships was not itself new, for they had featured in Jules Verne's and H. G. Wells's science fiction, and Leonardo da Vinci had designed one in the fifteenth century. It was mooted afresh in Britain during the winter of 1914–15 as the answer to the trench stalemate. When the War Office under Kitchener abandoned the idea after some unsuccessful trials with adapted tractors, the Admiralty took it up instead, thanks to the imagination and enthusiastic drive of Winston Churchill, the First Lord. On 26 March 1915 Churchill ordered the building of several prototype designs. Not until 26 January 1916, however, was a really practical 'tank' (the code name for the landship project) evolved and demonstrated in field tests. On hearing reports of the demonstration, GHQ in France ordered 40 tanks, later increased to 100. Henceforward, Haig counted on the tank to spearhead his Somme offensive. In the event, technical and production bottlenecks meant that the first tanks did not reach France until mid-August, and by mid-September there were still only 49 available. Nevertheless, Haig decided to launch them into battle. With the advantage of hindsight, critics have blamed him for not waiting until he could employ them en masse, which in fact would have meant waiting for another whole year. But the Allies were hoping that they might win the war in 1916. Haig therefore told the Chief of the Imperial General Staff in August: 'Even if I do not get so many as I hope, I shall use what I have got, as I cannot wait any longer for them, and it would be folly not to use any means at my disposal in what is likely to be our crowning effort for this year.'

On 15 September 1916 the weapon that was eventually to transform land warfare made its debut on a seven-and-a-half-mile front on the Somme. Owing to mechanical troubles, only 32 tanks actually took part in the offensive, clanking and grinding forward over the battlefield at a mere half a mile an hour, their interiors a hell of noise and heat; vehicles so clumsy that each needed a steering crew of four, and with armoured hull so crudely made that the impact of small-arms fire could flake lethal splinters from the inside surface.

Haig's instructions to his army commanders, Rawlinson of the Fourth Army and Sir Hubert Gough of the Fifth, called for 'bold action' and the maximum use of surprise. He wanted the tanks to be used in a concentrated punch in order to open a path right through the enemy defences for the infantry and cavalry. But Gough and Rawlinson bungled his purpose by ordering the customary preliminary bombardment, so both alerting the enemy and breaking up the ground, and by spreading the tanks out thinly along the fronts of their infantry divisions. Although the tanks enabled the British to make the deepest single advance of the whole battle and capture the fortified villages of Flers and Courcelette, the enemy quickly blocked the gap, and once again Haig was denied his grand breakthrough. Nevertheless, he was so impressed with the potential of the tank that he immediately asked the War Office to place an order for 1,000.

In response to urgent appeals from Joffre, the British army continued to attack grimly on through the rest of September, through October and into November. On 27 September the fortress-village of Thiepval on the left flank, one of the objectives for 1 July, fell at last; Beaumont-Hamel, another 1 July objective, not until 13 November. One by one regiments from every part of the United Kingdom – Scots, English, Irish, Welsh – had taken their turn in the battle; the rifle regiments; the Foot Guards; the Royal Marines. The Somme was a British Empire battle too. On the first day the Royal Newfoundland Regiment had lost 700 men out of 800. In July the South Africans fell thickly in Delville Wood; in September and October the Canadians, who had relieved the Australians round Pozières, fought their way two miles on towards Bapaume, while over to their right the New Zealanders attacked beyond the village of Flers. In November the Australians were back in the line for the last heave forward of all.

It was this final phase of the battle, in a slough of clinging, caramel-coloured mud, that fixed the lasting image of the Somme in British memory. Henry Williamson in his novel *A Patriot's Progress* (1930) describes the wounded coming back as he and his comrades moved up to the line:

> …men, single and in couples, shuffling past them, answering no questions. Tin hats on the backs of heads, no tin hats, tin hats with splinter-ragged, sandbagged coverings; men without rifles, haggard, bloodshot-eyed, slouching past in loose file, slouching on anyhow, staggering under rifles and equipment, some jaws sagging, puttees coiled mud-balled around ankles, feet in shapeless mud boots swelled beyond feeling, men slouching beyond fatigue and hope, on and on and on. G. S. [General Service] waggons with loads of sleeping bodies. Stretcher-bearers plodding desperate-faced.

Men slavering and rolling their bared-teeth heads, slobber-
ing and blowing, blasting brightness behind their eye-balls,
supported by listless cripples.

The British Empire was not fighting alone in the west. Throughout the battle a French army had been advancing on Haig's right
flank. And the Battle of Verdun was *still* going on. On 22 October,
after a three-day bombardment by artillery, the French launched
a counterstroke that led to the recapture of forts Vaux and
Douaumont.

Haig finally closed down his offensive on 18 November. On
15 December the French attacked for the last time at Verdun,
winning back another section of a battlefield which, wrote a French
corporal, 'resembled in places a rubbish dump in which there had
accumulated shreds of clothing, smashed weapons, shattered
helmets, rotting rations, bleached bones and putrescent flesh'.

So the great killing of 1916 came at last to its end. The cost to
both sides of 10 months of battle at Verdun amounted to some
700,000 killed and wounded, the French share of this total being
some 30–40,000 more than the German. The cost of four months
of battle on the Somme amounted to 415,000 British Empire
casualties and 195,000 French, while German casualties at least
equalled the combined Allied total. Excluding lightly wounded,
German losses for the year on all fronts came to 1,400,000 killed,
wounded and missing.

And still there was stalemate.

EIGHT

The German fleet assaults its jailer

COULD THE NAVIES BREAK THE DEADLOCK? On the morning of 31 May 1916, with the sun breaking through mist on a calm sea, the Commander-in-Chief of the Imperial German High Seas Fleet, Vice-Admiral Reinhard Scheer, set sail with the aim of enticing part of the British fleet into a trap and destroying it. Since becoming Commander-in-Chief in February, Scheer had persuaded the Kaiser that the German navy must adopt an aggressive policy instead of skulking in its ports. In the course of the previous year there had taken place only one clash between British and German heavy ships: the Battle of the Dogger Bank in the North Sea on 28 January, when signalling muddles in *Lion*, flagship of Sir David Beatty's Battle Cruiser Fleet, had enabled the outnumbered Admiral Franz von Hipper to escape with the loss of only one obsolete cruiser.

For all Scheer's justified confidence in his crews and ships, he had to recognize that with a total strength of only 18 modern battleships and five battle-cruisers against 31 British battleships and 10 battle-cruisers (fewer actually sailed to battle) he could not risk a general fleet action. His strategy was to dispatch Hipper's battle-cruisers north past the Danish territory of Jutland as a bait to draw down a portion of the British fleet. He himself, following with the battleships, would act as the trap. However, he did not know that the Admiralty had cracked the German naval code. Even before Scheer himself left Wilhelmshaven, Sir John Jellicoe and the whole Grand Fleet was at sea and steaming to intercept him. When Jellicoe reached the sea area off Jutland he, for his part, was unaware that Scheer had actually sailed, because Scheer had transferred his flagship's radio call sign to a shore station. On the afternoon of 31 May both fleets were running on in a fog of misinformation that complemented the treacherously shifting mists of the North Sea. Moreover, both admirals failed to make full use of their air components – seaplanes in the British case, Zeppelins in the German – for reconnaissance, but instead depended on their cruiser screens.

The fleets of the Great War, like the armies, reflected a technology in transition. Whereas Jellicoe's ships were 10 times heavier than Nelson's and could throw a projectile 10 times further, Jellicoe still depended, like Nelson, on masthead look-outs and even to a great extent on flag signalling. Like dinosaurs, the fleets were strong in armour and destructive power, weak in the sensory and control systems.

For Jellicoe and Scheer alike, a general action between modern battleships and their escorting cruisers and destroyers was an unknown quantity, a matter of conjecture, just as land fighting with modern weapons had been to the armies at the beginning of the

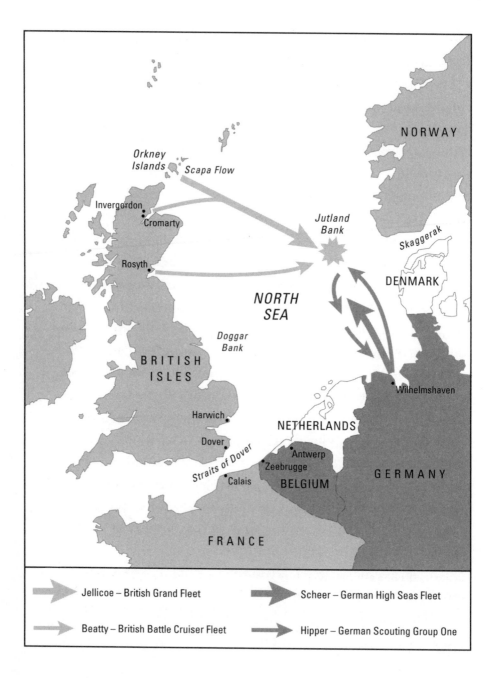

war. In particular Jellicoe expected torpedo attack by submarines or destroyers to offer a major threat to his battleships. Jellicoe also entertained well-founded misgivings about the comparative strength and hitting power of British and German ships. For these reasons – and also because after the long Victorian peace the Royal Navy had exchanged the Nelson touch for a habit of rigid obedience to centralized command – Jellicoe meant to avoid a Nelsonian direct attack and free-for-all, and instead engage the enemy in a single line ahead.

The Battle of Jutland, the only fleet action of the Great War, began at about 4 p.m. on 31 May 1916, when Beatty and the Battle Cruiser Fleet encountered Scheer's bait – five battle-cruisers under Hipper. When Hipper swung south to draw Beatty towards Scheer's battleships a high-speed running fight ensued. Owing to a misunderstanding, the strongest component of Beatty's force, four of the newest British battleships, was late to get into action. Superbly accurate German gunnery, coupled with weaknesses in the design of the British battle-cruisers, resulted in the loss of two out of Beatty's six battle-cruisers – *Indefatigable* and *Queen Mary* – blown up and sunk.

When Beatty's cruiser screen spotted Scheer's battleships ahead, it was Beatty's turn to act as bait, turning north and heading for Jellicoe and the Grand Fleet. Another running fight began in which

Opposite: **The Battle of Jutland, 31 May 1916.** Acting on a radio intercept, the Grand Fleet sailed to meet the German High Seas Fleet. The battle-cruisers clashed at 3.50 p.m. on 31 May; the main fleets about 6.30 p.m. After narrowly escaping destruction in three separate encounters in the mists, the German fleet steered for home during the night of 31 May–1 June.

the German battle-cruisers absorbed hit after hit from the 15-inch guns of Beatty's battleships without sinking.

Meanwhile Jellicoe, steaming into the mists with 24 battleships in six columns abeam, waited anxiously for exact information as to the strength, position and course of the enemy – facts on which his own deployment into line ahead absolutely depended. If he wrongly positioned his fleet he could, as Winston Churchill wrote later, lose the war in an afternoon. At 6.15 p.m. Beatty reported Scheer's position; two minutes later Jellicoe ordered the Grand Fleet to deploy into line behind his port (left-hand) wing column. He was just in time to cross Scheer's 'T' – in other words, Jellicoe's line stretched across the German path, enabling every British gun to bear on the enemy, while only the forward armament of the German ships could reply. In between the battle fleets the cruisers and destroyers were already fighting their own confused scrimmage. The funnel smoke of some 200 vessels belched into the mists.

For Scheer, not even aware that Jellicoe was at sea, the sudden spectacle of an interminable line of gun flashes in the mists ahead of him came as an appalling shock. It was he, not the British, who had been led into a trap. Only the defectiveness of British shell saved his leading ships from loss during the 10 minutes that elapsed before his fleet reversed course to the west, each vessel turning in its place. Yet that 10 minutes proved long enough for Hipper to blow up and sink yet another British battle-cruiser, the *Invincible*.

With the sudden vanishing of Scheer from British sight ended the first encounter between the main fleets at Jutland. Jellicoe did not turn to pursue, partly because he thought Scheer's disappearance was due to a temporary thickening of the mist, partly because he was resolved not to risk taking his battleships into a torpedo ambush. He held on round to the south to cut Scheer off from his base.

At 6.55 p.m. Scheer reversed course to the east again – and once more ran straight into Jellicoe's line. With his helpless ships again under a converging deluge of shell, the German Commander-in-Chief ordered another countermarch to the west, covering his retreat by a suicidal charge by his battered battle-cruisers and a torpedo attack by destroyers. Jellicoe, by turning *away* from the enemy in order to 'comb' the torpedo tracks instead of towards them, lost all chance of keeping contact. The firing died on the second fleet encounter of the battle.

Between about 8 p.m. and 9.30 p.m. the third indecisive clash took place, as the course of the two fleets, both now heading southwards, gradually converged. Despite sporadic long-range firing in the dying light, neither Jellicoe nor Beatty nor any British divisional commander endeavoured to steam straight for the enemy. The British line rigidly followed Jellicoe's centralized command; and Jellicoe did not intend to gamble with British mastery of the sea.

Since the Grand Fleet now lay between him and home, Scheer decided to smash his way through during the night hours. Luck favoured him, for the High Seas Fleet encountered only the British light forces astern of the Grand Fleet battleships. Despite the sound of heavy firing, Jellicoe did not alter course to intervene, for the Royal Navy was neither trained nor equipped for night fighting. Nor did he heed an Admiralty signal, based on a radio intercept, giving him Scheer's exact course home, which would have enabled him to steer so as to renew the battle at daybreak. The last of all the muddles of Jutland took place in the Admiralty itself, when further vital intercepted German signals giving Scheer's position were not relayed to Jellicoe at all. By 4.30 a.m. on 1 June the High Seas Fleet was safe at home in Wilhelmshaven.

The High Seas Fleet, though inferior in numbers at Jutland by 16 modern battleships to 28, and five battle-cruisers to nine, had sunk 111,980 tons of British warships and inflicted casualties of 6,945. The Grand Fleet had sunk 62,233 tons of German ships (including the badly damaged *Lützow*, sunk by the Germans themselves) and inflicted casualties of 2,921. The Germans were therefore quick to claim a victory, and the Fatherland rejoiced. An ineptly low-keyed Admiralty communiqué helped to plunge Britain into corresponding disappointment at the failure of her treasured navy to win another Trafalgar. The immediate moral effect of Jutland thus lay in Germany's favour. Technologically, too, Germany had had the best of it, for British heavy shell proved inferior in destructive power to German and British battle-cruisers inferior in defensive strength.

Nevertheless, Jutland served only to confirm that Britain's surface command of the sea was unshakeable. As an American journalist put it, 'The German Fleet has assaulted its jailer; but it is still in jail.' Scheer himself acknowledged that Jutland had been a strategic failure by recommending to the Kaiser that Germany's future main effort at sea must take the form of submarine warfare. Only the U-boat could answer the British blockade by counter-attacking British home morale and the British war economy.

At sea as on land, therefore, 1916 proved the year of deadlock; at sea as on land the only means to victory lay in the gradual attrition of the enemy's will and resources.

•

'HANS IS DEAD. FRITZ IS DEAD. WILHELM IS DEAD. There are many others. I am now quite alone in the company. God grant we may soon be relieved. Our losses are dreadful... If only peace would come!' Thus wrote a German soldier on the Somme. In the armies of all the combatants the slaughter of 1916 bequeathed a deep weariness and disillusion. The soldiers were no longer fighting for a patriotic ideal, like the volunteers of 1914, but because of the ties of comradeship forged within each section or platoon. Between them and the civilians back at home lay a gulf of mutual incomprehension. For the civilians, willingly feeding on romantic propaganda reports of 'victories' won by 'pluck' over a contemptible enemy, still thought of the fighting in the 'hurrah' style of 1914 – and the soldiers could not bring themselves to communicate the truth.

Many civilians also still burned with a hatred of the enemy that bordered on neurotic fantasy. A Briton pointed out in a newspaper, for example, that 'there are only two divisions in the world today – human beings and Germans', while a German argued on the contrary that 'The Englishman, indeed, is not to be classed among human beings'. Private journalism as well as official propaganda fanned these hatreds. The violent language of Horatio Bottomley's *John Bull*, which always referred to the enemy as 'the Germ-hun', was so appealing to the public that the journal achieved the largest circulation in Britain. The churches mobilized Christianity for war. A British bishop observed: 'Such a war is a heavy price to pay for our progress towards the realization of the Christianity of Christ, but duty calls.' The German religious interpretation naturally differed: 'One thing is clear. God must stand on Germany's side. We fight for truth, culture and civilization and human progress and true Christianity.'

Soldiers on leave were repelled by the frenetic pleasure-seeking of wartime London, Paris and Berlin. Restaurants and nightspots were thronged with those who were doing well out of munitions, war-profiteers stuffing themselves from menus that made a mockery of rationing and shortages. The wartime revolution in society and manners, so liberating in many respects, had its distinctly unlovely face.

Yet the home fronts too were beginning to feel the weight of total war. In Continental countries the cumulative losses of more than two years of mass battles had left hardly a family circle untouched; even in Britain, whose total casualties had been much smaller, bereavement was becoming appallingly commonplace. And life generally for the peoples at home was getting grimmer and greyer, as the war efforts swallowed up national resources, and the blockades of both sides began to pinch. The tonnage of shipping sunk by German U-boats rose from 108,000 in July 1916 to 325,100 in December. Although the Admiralty had experimented with 'Q' ships – heavily armed vessels disguised as helpless merchantmen – with occasional success, it had still found no real answer to the submarine. Britain depended on overseas supplies for over 60 per cent of her food. In November shortage of wheat forced the introduction of the coarser 'war bread' and patriots observed meatless days. The parks and commons of cities were dug up for growing vegetables. In December a Ministry of Food was set up to control all bulk supplies.

Britain, with her liberal traditions, still shrank from formal rationing. In Germany and Austria-Hungary, however, rationing of food and clothing had long become a glum fact of life, thanks to the Royal Navy's relentless blockade, which starved their agriculture of imported fertilizers. To the dreariness of the ration card and the queue was added that of the food substitute (ersatz), such as coffee made of roasted acorns, rice 'lamb' chops, vegetable 'beefsteak', limeflower tea, chemical substances for eggs and salad oil, synthetic fabrics and wooden-soled shoes.

For the civilians, as for the soldiers, the war had thus acquired the character of a grim permanent institution, a routine drudgery. The national unity forged in each country in the patriotic emotion of August 1914 was beginning to show cracks. In Britain at Easter 1916 Irish republicans rose in rebellion against British rule, and were crushed only after savage street fighting in Dublin and the execution of captured ringleaders. Yet in 1914 Irish nationalists at Westminster had volunteered support for Britain's cause. In Tsarist Russia a breakneck expansion of war industries had led to dangerous distortions in her economy, dangerous strains in her society. The new wartime Russian proletariat was beginning to fester with hunger and discontent.

Even in disciplined Germany the year had seen strikes in Berlin and in the Ruhr coalfields, food riots, Social Democrat opposition to the war in the Reichstag, and a peace demonstration by 30,000 workers in Frankfurt in October. In France war-weariness provided a rich breeding ground for pacifist propaganda and left-wing subversion. President Poincaré noted in November: 'There is everywhere, in the Parisian population and in the Chambers, a vague malaise. The "defeatists" are gaining ground every day... Suspicious miasmas float in the air.'

In this mood of emotional hangover after the bellicose intoxication of 1914–15 it was little wonder that some minds turned to the idea of a compromise peace as a means of escape from the calamitous predicament in which Europe found itself. In Britain the Union of Democratic Control, a mixed bag of Liberal, Labour and pacifist idealists, had long campaigned with little effect in favour of 'peace'. In November 1916 Lord Lansdowne, a member of the War Cabinet itself, wrote privately to his colleagues to ask whether a peace won by a continuation of the present slaughter and destruction would be worth the having.

It was the German government that on 12 December launched the first official peace move of the war, using the occupation of the Romanian capital of Bucharest a week earlier as a springboard. But the German note, while giving no hint as to terms, began tactlessly by asserting that Germany and her allies had 'gained gigantic advantages' in the field and could expect 'further successes'.

The truth was that only a section of the German Social Democrats favoured a peace without annexations. Chancellor Bethmann-Hollweg's own minimum terms included a Poland under German control, Belgium under German domination (with a German garrison in Antwerp) and the cession by France of the rich industrial area of Longwy-Briey. Even the so-called moderates in the Reichstag wanted a hardly smaller expansion of German power. Because of Germany's boasted 'gigantic advantages' at present occupying so much Allied soil, she would enjoy the bargaining leverage at a peace conference.

Here then, in German ambition and present outward success, lay the factors that ensured that in the event there would be no compromise peace, but a fight to the finish. The Allies, despite their weariness and disappointments, were by no means ready for peace on German terms, which would have rendered futile all their sacrifices thus far. Now, at the end of 1916, Britain, and to a lesser extent France, had completed immense programmes of industrial expansion for munitions production – national shell, explosives and shell-filling factories; aircraft and aero-engines manufacture; new chemical works; ball-bearing production; and a huge increase in electric power. Munitions of every kind were now flowing to the fighting front in vast quantities.

In January 1917 the US President Woodrow Wilson, in a vain attempt at mediation, asked both sides to state their war aims. Germany evaded a public answer; the Allies laid down conditions that foreshadowed the eventual Treaty of Versailles in 1919: evacuation of all occupied Allied territories; restoration of Belgium and Serbia; liberation of Czechs, Slavs, Romanians and other minorities from foreign rule. These were terms that, as the event proved, Germany would accept only in an hour of national defeat.

So the flurry of peace hopes blew away on the freezing winds of the coldest winter in memory. The nations came to a grim resolve to fight on. They put their trust in new leaders who would, they believed, find ways to end the deadlock and bring the boon of a victorious peace.

NINE

New leaders and fresh hopes

GHQ had to bear in mind that the enemy's great superiority in men and material would be even more painfully felt in 1917 than in 1916. They had to face the danger that Somme fighting would soon break out at various points on our fronts, and that even our troops would not be able to withstand such attacks indefinitely, especially if the enemy gave us no time for rest and for the accumulation of material... Our position was uncommonly difficult... If the war lasted our defeat seemed inevitable.

Thus wrote General Erich Ludendorff in his memoirs of Germany's plight in the autumn of 1916, the plight from which he, as 'First Quartermaster-General', and Field-Marshal Paul von Hindenburg, his chief, had to find an escape. In fact Ludendorff and Hindenburg were the first of the new national leaders brought to the top by the setbacks of 1916. It was natural that imperial Germany, dominated by the Prussian tradition of a military monarchy, should turn to soldiers for salvation. Hindenburg, Chief of Staff to the Kaiser and the figurehead to Ludendorff's executive brain, seemed the very embodiment of soldierly strength and virtue: tall, erect and massive, with close-cropped head and stern pouchy-eyed gaze over big moustaches. The German people worshipped him as if he were some hero with magic powers, reincarnated from ancient Teutonic legend.

In mid-September 1916 Ludendorff began the construction of an immensely powerful defence zone 25 miles behind the existing Somme front, called the Siegfried Position, but later dubbed by the British the 'Hindenburg Line'. The new shorter front, running across the base of the German bulge towards Amiens and Paris, would save 13 trench divisions. Yet the Hindenburg Line would not be completed until March 1917; until then Ludendorff was to watch with apprehension for signs of a renewed Allied offensive against his improvised trenches and exhausted troops on the Somme.

In order to match the swelling Allied resources in munitions, and also to compensate for German shortage of manpower by abundance of firepower, Ludendorff decided to double German war production – the so-called Hindenburg Programme. Since Ludendorff knew nothing about economics, the Hindenburg Programme took no account of the limitations of Germany's real resources, or of the basic needs of civilian life. Ludendorff mort-gaged Germany's ability to sustain a long war in order to obtain a huge boost in munitions in 1917. As with the Schlieffen Plan in

1914, purely military factors were allowed to dictate Germany's national policy; and just as in 1914, Germany needed a quick victory.

During the winter of 1916–17 – the 'turnip winter' in bitter German popular memory – the German leadership believed they had found the means to such a quick victory. Careful calculations by economic experts and the German naval staff seemed to prove that if the U-boat was allowed to sink all vessels at sight without warning instead of first identifying and sparing neutrals, then within a few months the British people would starve and British industry would come to a halt for want of raw materials. The German leadership recognized that such unrestricted submarine warfare would very probably provoke the United States to enter the war on the Allied side, but they calculated that the Atlantic sea lanes would have been cut and Britain defeated long before America could create a mass army and begin to transport it to France.

In January 1917, with Bethmann-Hollweg's peace initiative defunct, Germany proclaimed: 'From 1 February 1917 sea traffic will be stopped with every available weapon and without further notice in the following blockade zones...' The announcement went on to list the Western Approaches, the sea area around the British Isles, and the Mediterranean.

Thus, under her new leaders, Germany, still penned and surrounded by her enemies despite her conquests, sought escape from her predicament in yet another enormous gamble.

•

IN BRITAIN, FIELD-MARSHAL LORD KITCHENER – 'Kitchener of Khartoum' – had been the only soldier to attract the kind of hero worship enjoyed by Hindenburg; and his career, already in eclipse, had been finally snuffed out on 5 June 1916 when HMS *Hampshire*, carrying him on a mission to Russia, was sunk by a mine. Returning to their parliamentary traditions, the British people looked to a civilian leader to find a way out of the deadlock of autumn 1916: David Lloyd George, the Welshman whose energy, imagination and oratory while Minister of Munitions had brought about a veritable wartime industrial revolution. In the first week of December 1916 discontent among House of Commons backbenchers of all parties with Asquith's limp leadership led to a Cabinet crisis. On 6 December Lloyd George became War Premier, entrusted with the mission of dealing Germany 'the knock-out blow'.

Yet Lloyd George's position as head of a coalition government of all parties was nothing like as strong as that of Winston Churchill in the Second World War. Churchill was leader of the majority party in the Commons, while Lloyd George, himself a Liberal, depended on Conservative support. The Liberal Party itself had split, the majority remaining loyal to Asquith. The underlying weakness of Lloyd George's position had immediate and far-reaching consequences for British conduct of the war.

He came into office believing that the Somme battle had been a futile massacre and determined that there should not be another in 1917. A fresh offensive on the Western Front was the strategy advocated by Haig, the Commander-in-Chief of the British armies in France, and Sir William Robertson, the Chief of the Imperial General Staff. However, Lloyd George dared not provoke a showdown because Haig and Robertson enjoyed the confidence of his Conservative colleagues and of the King as well. Unable either to impose his own strategy on Haig and Robertson or to sack them, Lloyd George was to seek to curb their freedom of action by means of intrigue. It was the advent of a new leader in France that gave him his first opportunity.

•

IN NOVEMBER 1916 Allied military leaders, meeting at Chantilly under Joffre's chairmanship, had decided that the right strategy for 1917 was to renew the concentric squeeze on Germany and Austria on all fronts without giving the enemy a respite, the very strategy that Ludendorff most feared. On the Western Front the Anglo-French offensive on the Somme would be reopened at the beginning of February. In fact, although the Allies did not know it, this was some six weeks before the Hindenburg Line would be completed.

But Joffre too fell victim – like Falkenhayn, like Asquith – to the disappointments of 1916, and was replaced in December by General Robert Nivelle. Nivelle, one of the most junior generals in the French army, handsome and decisive of personality, eloquent in debate, had won a sudden reputation by his successful counterstrokes at Verdun. He and his military secretary, a gaunt and consumptive fanatic named d'Alenson, believed that they had found the elusive secret of the breakthrough. Instead of another battle of attrition on the Somme, as agreed at Chantilly, Nivelle proposed a grand offensive on the Aisne which he said would flood right through the German defences in hours, sweep deep across German communications and win the war outright in a few days. The French government put its faith in Nivelle as a sick man puts his faith in the miracle cure of a quack. Lloyd George too was captivated, since Nivelle (having an English mother) spoke English perfectly and far more eloquently than the inarticulate Haig and the taciturn Robertson, and because under the Nivelle Plan the main effort would fall on the French army.

The immediate drawback of the Nivelle Plan was that it meant the Allies would attack in April rather than the beginning of February because of the need for fresh preparations on the Aisne. Ludendorff was thus accorded the respite he so desperately needed.

On 26 February Lloyd George, Nivelle, Haig, Robertson and other Allied leaders met at Calais to discuss the mundane question of the breakdowns of the French rail system behind the British Front. Lloyd George, without consulting the War Cabinet or even the War Secretary, let alone Haig and Robertson, had in fact secretly colluded with Nivelle to have Haig and the British army directly subordinated to French command. At Lloyd George's invitation, Nivelle sprang this proposal soon after the conference began, to the fury and dismay of the British delegates. In the face of angry opposition by Haig and Robertson, a compromise formula was finally evolved whereby Haig would come under Nivelle's command for the duration of the coming offensive only, and would have the right of appeal to his own government if he believed his army was endangered by French orders.

Lloyd George's manoeuvre, largely unsuccessful though it

proved, served to destroy all trust between himself and his senior military colleagues when his war premiership was yet in its infancy. The resulting deep mutual suspicion between the 'Brasshats' and the 'Frocks' [frock-coats] was to bedevil British decision-making for the rest of the war, with potentially catastrophic consequences.

In France too the political and military leaderships were riven with intrigue and mistrust. Pétain, now an army group commander, believed that Nivelle's hope of a quick breakthrough and a war-winning victory in the field was a fantasy; so too did General Joseph Micheler, commanding the army group responsible for the coming offensive. On 17 March the Prime Minister, Alexandre Ribot, who had backed Nivelle, fell. The strong-minded Minister of War in the new government, Paul Painlevé, shared the doubts about Nivelle's plan. Nivelle, harried by his critics, took refuge in a stubborn optimism – even after the German retreat to the Hindenburg Line, which began on 15 March, virtually obliterated the bulge Nivelle had been hoping to cut off.

While a searingly cold winter turned reluctantly to a spring of snow and sleet and chilling rain, the French army readied itself for one last great effort. Critics believed that even the huge total of 7,000 guns was not enough to smash a German defence organized in great depth along a 40-mile front; they believed too that the tactical plan for the infantry advance was too rigid. So lax was security that rumours of the plan and the launch date were buzzing about the dinner tables of Paris and even London.

It was a former French Minister of War, now commanding a division on the front of the coming offensive, Paul Messimy, who brought the growing misgivings to a head by sending a personal note to the French Prime Minister. On 6 April a Council of War was held at GHQ Compiègne in the presence of the President of the Republic, Poincaré. The embattled Nivelle refused to concede the arguments of critics like Pétain and Micheler, and offered his resignation. The French government now had a clear duty to back Nivelle or sack him. It did neither; it limply left him to get on with it. Nivelle had to launch his offensive knowing that he enjoyed the confidence of neither his military colleagues nor his government, and that the price of failure would be his own head.

Thus the new national leaderships in Berlin, London and Paris failed to match the qualities of superhuman wisdom and courage hopefully credited to them by their peoples, or to grasp the magnitude of the calamity that had overtaken Europe.

•

THREE DAYS AFTER THE FRENCH COUNCIL OF WAR AT COMPIÈGNE, Haig, as agreed with Nivelle, launched an offensive at Arras in order to divert German reserves and attention from the Aisne. By contrast with the disastrous first day of the Somme, the assault forces (little smaller than on the Somme and on only a slightly narrower front) captured the German second line with little difficulty, and suffered only 32,000 casualties in the first three days as against 70,000 in the first three days of the Somme battle. It was proof of how much the British army and its command had learned in the hard school of experience. The Canadians swept up the long slope of Vimy Ridge and over the crest, where the crater field can still be seen today under the soft grass. Once the initial setpiece attack behind a creeping barrage was over, the Battle of Arras degenerated into the usual pattern of costly and indecisive slogging, in this case kept going only to support Nivelle.

Meanwhile, along the Aisne, the packed French divisions waited and shivered in the unseasonable sleet of early April, the dark faces of the Moroccan and Senegalese troops, summoned from the French Empire to replace France's own lost youth, drained grey by the cold. The French guns pounded the German defence zone along the Chemin des Dames Ridge, a maze of wire and interlocking fire three positions deep. French spirits were high: 'We are playing our last cards,' ran one unit order. 'A higher courage than ever is demanded of all.'

At 6 a.m. on 16 April 1917 the Nivelle offensive began. The élan of the troops was undoubted; the standard of staff work and coordination of artillery, infantry and airpower slapdash. Instead of the expected effortless flood straight through the German defence – 'Laon in twenty-four hours and then the pursuit' Nivelle had promised – the offensive achieved only limited gains of the customary kind. The Germans, following a new tactical method, launched large-scale counterstrokes once the attackers had lost their cohesion and momentum in the defensive maze. Although Nivelle had promised he would call off the offensive immediately if it failed to achieve a breakthrough, the fighting dragged on for 10 days. France's last effort, the offensive that was to win the war, resulted in a gain of some four miles at a cost of over 180,000 casualties.

The failure shattered Nivelle's fragile reputation, and on

17 May he gave place to Pétain, the realist who believed in fire-power rather than military rhetoric.

•

GERMAN HOPES OF WINNING THE WAR IN 1917 were likewise falsified by the course of events. At first the U-boats, relieved of the obligation to stop and identify ships as enemy or neutral, achieved the rate of sinking predicted by the experts. In February 540,000 tons of merchant shipping were sunk; in March 593,000; in April the astonishing total of 881,000 tons. The British First Sea Lord, Admiral Jellicoe, warned the War Cabinet: 'It is impossible for us to go on with the war if losses like this continue.' He also added that the Admiralty could see no answer to the U-boat at that present time.

Some 5,000 German sailors in about 100 frail submersible craft, a tiny fraction of the prodigious German war effort, had thus brought the world's greatest maritime power within sight of total national catastrophe.

By July sinkings had dropped back to 557,900 tons; by September to only 351,700 tons. These figures spelled defeat for the U-boat. The cause of this swift reversal of fortune was the convoy system adopted in May, largely owing to pressure by Lloyd George on a reluctant Admiralty. Instead of preying on lone and helpless merchant ships the U-boats now had to face counter-attack by escorting warships, detection by the new hydrophone listening gear (Asdic) and destruction by depth charges. Even a near miss could split a U-boat's pressure hull like a nutshell in the crackers.

There was another and less obvious reason for the success of the convoy system. No longer was merchant shipping scattered along the Atlantic trade routes to provide abundant targets for the roving U-boat, but instead gathered in relatively few groups of up to 50 vessels. Each U-boat now found the horizon emptied of shipping; she might cruise for days without sighting a victim. If she did encounter a convoy her limited underwater speed would enable her to attack only one or two vessels before the convoy steamed on out of range.

By the autumn, therefore, Germany's great war-winning gamble for 1917 had failed. Now Germany had to face the heavy consequences – the inevitable arrival of an American army in France in strength in 1918. For, just as had been foreseen in Berlin, unrestricted submarine warfare had provoked the United States into declaring war on Germany. Yet less than a month before this declaration of war on 6 April 1917 there occurred an event that rendered needless the fateful German gamble on the U-boat: the outbreak of revolution in Tsarist Russia, which paralysed the formidable enemy of Germany and Austria on the Eastern Front.

TEN

A disorderly mob bearing red flags

ON 8 MARCH 1917, a cold diamond-bright morning in the Russian capital Petrograd (the Russian form of the Germanic 'St Petersburg', patriotically adopted in August 1914), queues waiting outside food shops for flour erupted into riot. In the following days the streets filled with people, milling about almost as if on holiday. Food riots and street demonstrations being no novelty in a Europe at war, the Tsar Nicholas II left his capital for GHQ without a qualm. On 11 March the Petrograd authorities decided to clear the streets with armed police and troops. The French ambassador observed what followed from the window of his room:

> I heard a strange and prolonged din, which seemed to come from the Alexander Bridge. Almost immediately, a disorderly mob, carrying red flags, appeared at the end which is on the right bank of the Neva, and a regiment

came towards it from the opposite end. It looked as though there would be a violent collision, but on the contrary, the two bodies coalesced; the army was fraternising with the revolt.

Next day the demonstration exploded into revolution. The Petrograd garrison of 190,000 men, even units of the Imperial Guard, joined the angry crowds, which proceeded to storm the Winter Palace, burn public buildings and release political prisoners from the Russian 'Bastille', the Fortress of St Peter and St Paul. Michael Rodzianko, the President of the Duma (the Russian Parliament), frantically telegraphed the Tsar to plead for timely reforms: 'The final hour has come when the fate of the country and the dynasty must be decided.' Nicholas II, with a foolish arrogance typical of him, observed: 'This fat Rodzianko has sent me some nonsense to which I will not even reply.'

The Duma, hitherto a virtually impotent talking shop, now ignored a decree for its dissolution issued by the Prime Minister, Prince Golitzin, and set up an all-party committee to restore public order. In Moscow, as throughout Russia, this assumption of power was greeted with 'compelling, almost infectious enthusiasm', according to the British Consul-General. When the Tsar turned to the army in order to reassert his personal rule, the troops he dispatched to Petrograd simply joined the insurgents. As General Brusilov recorded later, 'The whole army was ready for a revolution.'

Thus, in a mere week, the Tsar's moral and physical authority had crumbled to nothing. Unable even to return to his capital

Below The third Battle of Ypres 1917, popularly known as 'Passchendaele'. Australian troops passing over a duckboard track at Château Wood.

Below An aerial view of trenches west of Auchy-lez-la-Bassée. Craters left by British mines are clearly visible, as is a shell exploding in the white chalk of no-man's-land. **Opposite top** Jacking and hauling a field gun out of the mud north of Ypres during the Battle of Pilckem Ridge, August 1917. The wet weather conditions made the battlefield at Ypres an immense bog. **Opposite bottom** On 7 November 1917 (25 October by the Russian calendar then in use) Communists seized the railway stations, bridges and communication centres in Petrograd.

Previous pages The workshop at Roehampton where artificial limbs were constructed for the wounded.
Above French soldiers relaxing at the front.
Right Rats prospered and multiplied in the trenches.

Below left Britain's first fighter ace, Captain Albert Ball, at the age of 20. He usually flew a Nieuport Scout. **Below right** Germany's Baron Manfred von Richthofen was called the 'Red Baron' because he flew a scarlet Fokker triplane. **Bottom** A church in Hull suffers damage as a result of enemy air raids.

Below Women workers doping the canvas covering of aircraft wings. **Bottom** Members of the Women's Forage Corps feeding a hay baler.

because peasants had torn up the railway, he abdicated at Pskov on 15 March in favour of his brother Michael – who never took up the crown. The 300-year-old Romanov dynasty had fallen, the first but by no means the last dynastic victim of the Great War.

The explosive social forces detonated by the Petrograd food riots had been long building up. Since 1914 Russia had been creating an immense new industrial capacity, so that by the end of 1916 she was able to supply her armies with all the weapons and ammunitions they needed. The effect of such a wartime industrial boom on an otherwise backward economy of peasant agriculture, poor communications and incompetent bureaucracy was dangerously lopsided, bringing economic and social strain. Thanks to the boom, Russia's urban proletariat increased by about a third between 1914 and 1917, rootless millions living in close-packed slums. Yet the peasants failed to supply the grain surpluses needed to feed the swelling towns. The incompetence of the railway administration and the effects of the harsh winter of 1916–17 did the rest. With a griping shortage of food and the cost of living some 600 per cent above the 1914 level, distress and discontent seethed, to the profit of left-wing agitators.

The prosperous middle classes too had become alienated from the Tsarist autocracy. Nicholas II, weak but vain, had been egged on by his Tsarina and her confidant, the lecherous and drunken monk Rasputin, to preserve intact the personal rule of his forebears. He had therefore denied the middle classes a share in the running of the country. Thus condemned to impotence, the middle and upper classes could only criticize in angry frustration the corruption and incompetence of the Tsar's administration.

The very first act of rebellion against Nicholas II had been the murder of Rasputin by a group of nobles in 1916.

The army, peasants in uniform, had lost all faith in the Tsar and his agents because of the chaos of military administration and because of its own appalling cumulative losses since 1914, the highest of any belligerent. It was rations of rotten herring rather than defeat (for the Russian army had successfully taken the offensive in 1916 under Brusilov) that had brought the soldiers to the present point of mutiny. By March 1917, therefore, all sections of the nation were sick of the Tsar and all he stood for.

Now, with Nicholas II gone, the Russian people, 190,000,000 strong, stood at a crossroads of history. It seemed at that moment that they would follow the path of Western parliamentary democracy. The Duma elected a provisional government of moderates under the liberal Prince Lvov, with a single Social Revolutionary (or Socialist), Alexander Kerensky, a lawyer, as Minister of Justice. The new regime faced a formidable rival for power in the Petrograd Soviet (the Russian word for 'council'), a group of Marxist politicians claiming to represent factory workers and soldiers. On 17 March the Soviet issued 'Order Number One' to the army, by which each unit was to elect a soldiers' council. Authority in the army began to pass from the officers, who were now alleged to be the class enemies of the rank and file, to the soldiers' councils. In order to allow this process of disruption in the Russian army to continue unhindered, the German high command deliberately abstained from attacking on the Eastern Front. With a cunning ultimately to rebound on their own heads, they gave secret passage across Germany in a sealed train to the notorious Communist agitator, Lenin, hitherto in exile in Switzerland. Nicolai Lenin, a man of ruthless ambition, and with a long-meditated blueprint for revolution and the achievement of a dictatorship of the proletariat, immediately became the dominating force in the Petrograd Soviet. He and his associates preached what a weary army and people most desired: the conclusion of an immediate peace, no matter on what terms.

The provisional government, however, pursued the very opposite policy towards the war. It proclaimed that it would 'loyally maintain its alliances and do everything in its power to carry the war to a victorious conclusion'.

To Britain and France the fall of the Tsar seemed to bode nothing but good, for they counted on the new democratic Russia to wage war with fresh enthusiasm and efficiency. As Lloyd George declared in the House of Commons: 'We believe that the revolution is the greatest service the Russian people have yet made to the cause for which the Allied peoples have been fighting.'

By an ironic paradox, therefore, both Germany and Austria on the one hand and France, Britain and Italy on the other looked with hope that spring to the future course of events in Russia.

·

ON 2 APRIL 1917 President Woodrow Wilson went to Capitol Hill in Washington to ask Congress to make war on the German Empire. With his own brand of high-minded eloquence he told his hearers:

To such a task we can dedicate our lives and our fortunes, everything that we are and everything we have, with the pride of those who know that the day has come when America is privileged to spend her blood and her might for the principles that gave her birth and happiness and the peace which she has treasured. God helping her, she can do no other.

For three years Wilson had clung to neutrality, even proclaiming that America was 'too proud to fight'. In this policy he reflected a deep national tradition, running back to the very founding of the Republic, that the United States should never let herself become involved in European power struggles. Since then each emigrant to America had, by the very fact of emigrating, proclaimed his personal rejection of Europe. Americans cherished the myth that, isolated from the taints of Europe's corrupt institutions by the broad Atlantic, they were creating a new kind of society, more free, more equal and more happy.

Even after Germany began unrestricted submarine warfare on 1 February 1917, Congress still refused to sanction the arming of merchant vessels, and Wilson had to order this under his executive authority as President. But when in March U-boats sank five American ships with the loss of American lives, public opinion began swiftly to harden against Germany. It took a further and incredibly stupid stroke of German policy to push America over the brink. The German Foreign Office decided to exploit an acrimonious territorial dispute between the United States and Mexico by proposing an alliance to Mexico. As an inducement, Germany offered the eventual restoration of territories lost by Mexico to America in the nineteenth century – New Mexico, Texas and Arizona. This crude attempt to stir up a conflict on America's own doorstep, in clear breach of the Monroe Doctrine, was decoded by the British Admiralty and made public, causing a wave of anger even in the more isolationist regions of the United States. On 6 April, the United States declared war, pledged in Wilson's words to use 'force to the uttermost, force without stint or limit'.

Thus, less than a month after the Russian Revolution, began that American involvement with the destinies of Europe which, except for a brief period in the 1930s, has continued ever since.

For the Allies this was a moment of surging hope. When General John J. Pershing, Commander-in-Chief of the American Expeditionary Force, visited Europe in June the crowds greeted him with near hysteria and pelted him with roses. American belligerence added to the scales of war a population of 93,400,000 and an annual steel production which, at 45,060,607 tons, was three times larger than that of Germany and Austria together. Yet in purely military terms America was at present only weak. How long would it be before the tiny American regular army could be expanded into a great field force, trained and equipped, transported across the Atlantic and deployed in Europe? Apart from the provision of American warships to make up the British shortage of escort vessels, it would be many, many months before America's entry into the war made a great impact. In the gloomy aftermath of Nivelle's failure, the British and French leaderships had to make up their minds as to the best strategy to follow in the meantime.

•

THE NEW FRENCH COMMANDER-IN-CHIEF, General Philippe Pétain, came to his post in May convinced that victory must now depend on the arrival of the Americans in strength in 1918. The exhausted French army would launch no more grand offensives meanwhile, but limit itself to a series of meticulously prepared setpiece local offensives, each supported by enormous weight of firepower, and with strictly limited objectives and duration. By such a strategy Pétain hoped to spare his soldiers, retain the initiative and inflict disproportionate casualties on the enemy. However, only three days after he took up his command the first reports reached him of serious mutinies in the French army.

•

FROM THEN TILL THE MIDDLE OF JUNE fresh outbreaks of disaffection were to occur at the rate of seven or eight a day, until 55 divisions, half the French army, had been affected. In almost every case the mutinies took place in units in rest camps behind the lines – units that had taken part in Nivelle's offensive. It was some comfort to Pétain that troops in the trenches remained staunch, valiantly resisting German counter-attacks. The outbreaks followed a pattern: on receiving orders to return to the line, the soldiers would gather in a crowd to shout defiance at their officers, or stage protest marches in which the singing of the Communist anthem, 'The Internationale', alternated with shouts of 'Leave!' and 'We won't go up the line!' In one camp a brigadier was howled down and manhandled; in another the officers were stoned and the commanding officer's house shot at. One unit took the road to Paris, only to be rounded up by cavalry like straying bullocks;

another hid for three days in a wood; yet others refused to leave their huts to go on parade, threatening to fire on anyone who disturbed them. As the mutinies spread, there were more ominous reminders of events in Russia, for some units elected 'soldiers' delegates' to voice their demands to the officers, and there was excited talk of a march on Paris.

Yet, though agitators were busy among the mutineers, the causes of the mutinies lay deeper than left-wing propaganda, deeper even than that bitter sense of disappointment after the extravagant hopes raised by Nivelle which had supplied the actual trigger for the outbreaks. The French soldier had, quite simply, been ill used too long; his loyalty had been tried too far. French military administration still owed much to the slapdash 'muddle-through' tradition of Napoleon's day. Unlike the British or German soldier, the *poilu* could not be sure of adequate and regular hot food or even good medical care, let alone the kind of canteens and recreational facilities found behind the British Front. His so-called rest camps were military slums. The French regimental officer was far less closely concerned with his soldiers' health and welfare than the British or German officer. In his misery, the *poilu* turned to free-issue *pinard* (rot-gut red wine), with even worse effects on morale and discipline.

With a blend of firmness, patience and understanding, Pétain gradually mastered the mutinies and set about reforming abuses. The danger of total disintegration did not pass until mid-June. At the same time the collapse of the hopes of peace through victory peddled by Nivelle brought the French people themselves to a weariness verging on despair. There was a wave of strikes and industrial protest, exploited as in Russia by political extremists. The Minister of the Interior, Louis Malvy, himself a Radical Socialist, made no attempt to combat revolutionary or pacifist agitation. His own circle included Bolo Pasha, a political go-between in German pay, and Eugène Almereyda, the editor of the pacifist and revolutionary paper *Le Bonnet Rouge*. Thanks to Malvy's protection, *Le Bonnet Rouge* still received a French government subsidy while it was carrying paid German propaganda. Revolutions were a hallowed French tradition; in the summer of 1917, with the *Union Sacrée* in tatters and shouting demonstrators thronging Paris streets, yet another one seemed all too possible.

•

SIR DOUGLAS HAIG BELIEVED – with some justification – that the British Empire forces under his command constituted the most formidable field army remaining on the Allied side, and one perfectly capable of defeating the Germany army in a great battle. On 1 May, following the collapse of Nivelle's hopes, Haig sent the War Cabinet a memorandum on 'The Present Situation and Future Plans', advocating a major offensive from the Ypres Salient aimed first at capturing the German rail junction of Roulers and then at sweeping northeastwards to the frontier of neutral Holland. The memorandum signalled the beginning of three months of anguished strategic debate, in which the old gulf between the 'Brass-hats' and the 'Frocks' opened wider still.

ELEVEN

They called it Passchendaele

'A CORRECT DECISION was not so easy to make at the time as it appears now,' wrote Sir William Robertson after the war about the projected Flanders offensive. It was a just comment. So many factors lay misted in uncertainty. Would Russia stay in the war? Gloomy reports by Allied observers with the Russian army contradicted earlier optimism about Russia's new regime. What of France? Pétain categorically promised Haig French military support. Even though the French carefully concealed from their ally the full appalling dimensions of the mutinies in their army, the British were well aware that France and her army were suffering a severe crisis of morale. Could Pétain's promises be depended on? The enemy was also having his strikes and demonstrations; how near to breaking point was his own will to wage war? Then there was the U-boat. Admiral Jellicoe warned the War Cabinet in June that with the then rate of merchant-ship losses it was pointless

even to think about 1918, and urged the vital importance of elim-
inating the U-boat bases along the Belgian coast.

Haig argued that his proposed offensive offered the best strategic answer to all these puzzles. It would encourage the Russians.
It would give French hope, in his words, 'something to feed on'
during the long interval before the Americans arrived in force. It
would clear the Belgian coast. If all went well and the British
advance reached the Dutch frontier, it might even, Haig contended, induce Germany to make peace in 1917. On the basis of
the six-mile advance at Arras in April and a successful capture
of the Messines Ridge on 7 June, Haig was confident that he had
solved the technical problem of the breakthrough.

Lloyd George, in relentlessly cross-examining Haig and
Robertson, expressed profound doubts as to whether such a breakthrough could be achieved, and fears lest the British army should
be sucked into another Somme battle. He advocated instead that
on the Western Front the Allies should do little more than wait for
the Americans, while transferring a mass of artillery to support
Italian offensives against Austria. 'If the Germans came to the
assistance of the Austrians, then you would be fighting them and
wearing them out,' he told the War Policy Committee of the
Cabinet in June. He cynically added: 'But this would take place
at the expense of the Italians and not our own men.' Haig and
Robertson, the 'Westerners', contended, however, that this
'Easterner's' strategy would dangerously weaken the Western Front
while inflicting little or no damage on the main enemy, Germany.

Through May, June and July the argument revolved without
a decision, even though – with Cabinet sanction – the vast

preparations for the Flanders offensive continued, including the start of the preliminary bombardment itself on 15 July. No meeting of minds took place, but instead a sterile confrontation between sides that deeply mistrusted each other. Finally, on 20 July, the War Cabinet authorized Haig 'to carry out the plans for which he has prepared'. For even though Lloyd George remained totally opposed to the offensive, he had in the end shrunk from asserting the Cabinet's constitutional responsibility over British strategy.

Thus unsatisfactorily ended perhaps the most crucial British strategic debate of the war; and thus the army of the British Empire came to be committed to the experience ever after to be remembered as 'Passchendaele', the name of the final objective attained, and one of those assigned to the first day.

The main offensive was preceded by an attack to secure its southern flank by capturing the strong German position on the Messines Ridge. Mounted by the Second Army under Sir Herbert Plumer, it was a masterpiece of meticulous organization. On 7 June, 19 huge mines that had been two years in secret underground preparation exploded beneath the German defences, and the infantry went in behind a creeping barrage from 2,330 guns and howitzers. By the end of the day the whole ridge lay in British hands, and the Germans had lost 24,000 men and 67 guns to British losses of 17,000 killed, wounded and missing. It seemed a brilliant omen for the coming Third Battle of Ypres.

Haig's plan for this fell into two phases. He would first strike northeast from the Ypres Salient and seize a rim of high ground running from Staden through Passchendaele and Gheluvelt.

Then, in conjunction with a seaborne landing near Nieuport (cancelled in the event), he would drive north towards Ostend and Bruges, with the Dutch frontier as his ultimate objective. He hoped at least to get as far as the railway line Roulers–Thourout, 12 miles behind the German Front. Because he hoped for a rapid advance he gave command of the offensive to General Sir Hubert Gough and the Fifth Army, Gough being the youngest army commander and enjoying a reputation as a thruster, rather than to Plumer, the expert in set pieces.

The offensive was dogged with ill-fortune from the start. Haig had originally hoped that massed tanks would enable him to break through without the need for a massive preliminary bombardment that would smash up the ground, but owing to continued production difficulties, only 150 were available in July. A bombardment there had to be. Since the offensive had been delayed some months beyond the date first envisaged by Haig because of the changes in Allied commanders and plans since Joffre's dismissal, it now happened to coincide with the wettest August for years. The combination of a huge weight of artillery fire and drenching rain proved disastrous. With all the ditches and land drains destroyed, the battlefield became an immense bog.

For the British command the results of the first day's assault on 31 July offered a perplexing picture of partial success. While the left wing had advanced some two miles, the centre and right had finished up less than half way to their objective, the Passchendaele-Gheluvelt ridge. For the enemy had once again sprung his own surprises: a new system of defence in depth, shell-proof concrete bunkers, and powerful counter-attack groups that struck the attackers at the moment of maximum exhaustion and disarray.

Although Haig ordered Gough to continue attacking, the incessant rain delayed further action until 10 August, when the British failed again to capture the Gheluvelt Plateau. After another vain floundering forward in the mud at Langemarck on 16 August, Gough advised Haig that tactical success was impossible and the offensive should be abandoned. Haig believed that if only the weather improved there was still a chance of clearing the Belgian coast before autumn, and that in any case the general war situation demanded that the British army should grip the enemy by the throat. The British were not fighting alone. On 17 August the Italian army under Count Luigi Cadorna launched the *eleventh* battle of the Isonzo; three days later Pétain carried out at Verdun the first of his promised limited operations, with complete success. The apparently futile attacking through the mud at Ypres was having its effect on the defenders. Ludendorff wrote in his memoirs:

> The costly August battles in Flanders and at Verdun imposed a heavy strain on the western troops. In spite of all the concrete protection they seemed more or less powerless under the enormous weight of the army's artillery. At some points they no longer displayed that firmness which I, in common with the local commanders, had hoped for.

At the end of August Haig transferred command of the battle from Gough to Plumer. The weather changed; September proved fine and dry. Plumer and his outstandingly able Chief of Staff,

Charles Harrington, organized three of their meticulous set-piece attacks (Menin Road Ridge, Polygon Wood and Broodseinde) during this month and the first week of October. At the Menin Road Ridge there were 1,295 guns, one to every five yards of front, the largest concentration ever achieved by the British army. The rolling barrage in front of the troops was 1,000 yards deep, composed of five separate belts of fire. The infantry occupied the area swept clean of the enemy by the guns, and then the huge battering engine was laboriously hauled forward and set up for the next advance. At the climax of the Battle of Broodseinde on 4 October, the advancing Australians saw green fields – the German rear areas – beckoning.

Then the rain fell again – 'our most effective ally' in the words of Crown Prince Rupprecht of Bavaria, the defending German army group commander. The battlefield dissolved into porridge. The army of the British Empire still struggled on – all through October and into November. Believing with some reason that the enemy was strained to the limit, Haig, a man of inflexible will, would not give up, even though the general feeling of his army commanders was against him; even though he was very well aware that the battlefield was a swamp that swallowed men, guns and machines. This last stage of the Third Battle of Ypres provided the scenes of the nightmare that inspired some of the most deeply felt of all war poetry. Wilfred Owen called the battlefield:

> *...a sad land (weak with sweats of death)*
> *Grey, cratered like the moon with hollow woe*
> *And pitted with great pocks and scabs of Plagues.*

And Siegfried Sassoon wrote:

...I died in hell
(They called it Passchendaele) my wound was slight
And I was hobbling back; and then a shell
Burst slick upon the duckboards; so I fell
Into the bottomless mud, and lost the light.

In the October fighting the Australians and New Zealanders struggled nearly to the crest of the Passchendaele Ridge before being withdrawn, utterly spent. Passchendaele itself, now no more than a brick-coloured smear in the welter of cratered mud, fell to the Canadians on 20 November. Six days later Haig closed down the Third Battle of Ypres at last.

Measured against Haig's own stated prior intentions, the offensive must be accounted a complete failure. The losses were, so far as can be guessed amid uncertain and disputed statistics, about equal at around 250,000 killed, wounded and missing on each side. It is impossible to judge which side suffered the greater moral damage, for both emerged exhausted and deeply shaken. Sir Philip Gibbs, a famous war correspondent, recorded: 'For the first time the British army lost its sense of optimism, and there was a sense of deadly depression among many officers and men with whom I came in touch.' Yet perhaps it was worse for the Germans, forced slowly but inexorably back. Ludendorff wrote: 'The troops had borne the continuous defensive with extreme difficulty... they thought with horror of fresh defensive battles and longed for a war of movement.' By gripping the German

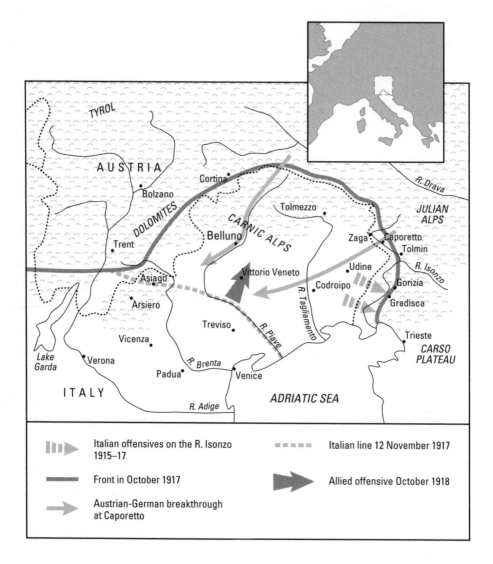

Above: **The Italian Front 1915–18.**

army so remorselessly for more than four months (as many as 73 German divisions rotated through the battle), Haig certainly gave Pétain the respite he needed to restore the French army to health.

Perhaps the most important consequence of Third Ypres lay far in the future – in the 1920s and 1930s – when the image of futile slaughter printed on the public mind by the war writers and poets was to cause a wave of pacifist feeling in Britain that helped to prevent timely rearmament against Hitler's Germany.

•

FOR ALL THE STRAIN ON THE GERMAN ARMY in the west exerted by Haig's remorseless massed artillery, Ludendorff managed to preserve a central strategic reserve of seven crack divisions for use on any front. In August the Austrian Chief of Staff (now Baron Artur Arz von Straussenburg) asked Germany to relieve Austrian divisions on the Russian Front because he wished to concentrate a striking force for a great counterstroke against the Italians. Instead, Ludendorff dispatched his own strategic reserve to the Italian Front so that German generals and German soldiers could lead the offensive.

In contrast to the Western Front, the Italian Front traced its way through 400 miles of tumbled mountainside. Only the extreme eastern sector of about 50 miles along the River Isonzo had invited attack by the Italian army, partly because the terrain here rose to 'only' 8,000 feet, partly because 15 miles beyond the Isonzo lay the great Austrian naval base of Trieste. The 1,000-foot plateau of the Carso, where some of the bitterest fighting took place, had its own special horror – shells and small-arms fire sent lethal or blinding splinters flying from its limestone surface. The Italian army's 11 offensives on the Isonzo had finally taken it half way to Trieste at a total cost of over a million casualties. The last and biggest such offensive, in August and September 1917, proved the Italian equivalent of the Nivelle offensive, for it brought the Italian infantry (even worse cared for by way of food, medical care and welfare than the French) to the edge of moral collapse. Yet Austrian army commanders reported that their own men could not stand up to further Italian attacks, and it was this that decided Arz von Straussenburg to gamble on a counterstroke.

After a brief hurricane bombardment, the counter-offensive, planned and led by the German General Otto von Below and his Chief of Staff Krafft von Delmensingen, smashed home on 24 October 1917 in rain, snow and low cloud on the Caporetto sector, north of the main Isonzo battlefield. The attackers infiltrated swiftly through the Italian positions, advancing about 12 miles in the day; in an outstanding exploit, Oberleutnant Erwin Rommel led his mountain troops to the peak of one of three 6,000-foot mountains that formed the bastion of the Italian defence. The Italian Second Army, a formation poor in discipline and morale, collapsed in utter rout. The German-Austrian army surged down into the plain, across the communications of the Italian forces on the Isonzo front, which now struggled westward to escape the trap. The Italian Commander-in-Chief, Luigi Cadorna, managed to establish a fresh defence only 15 miles east of Venice, behind the wide river Piave. He had lost 10,000 killed, 30,000 wounded and 293,000 in prisoners, while 400,000 deserters had melted away into towns and villages. The Battle of Caporetto had proved the most spectacular victory of the war since Gorlice-Tarnów in 1915.

•

ON 1 SEPTEMBER another German army, under Oskar von Hutier, an outstanding field commander, struck at the Russian defence covering Riga on the Baltic. The short hurricane bombardment was masterminded by Germany's greatest artillery expert, Colonel Bruchmüller. The German onslaught, pressed home with ruthless speed, tore the Russian defence apart like an old curtain; Riga fell within a few hours. Ludendorff, however, had a grander objective in mind than this naval base – no less than delivering a fatal shock to Russia's tottering provisional government.

Alexander Kerensky had been the soul of this government, first as Minister of Justice, then as Minister of War and, after 21 July, as Prime Minister. A wildly romantic idealist, he sought to emulate the leaders of the French Revolution and stir up a new national spirit of resistance through sheer oratory. In Galicia on 1 July the Russian army had launched its last offensive of the war – dubbed 'the Kerensky offensive' or 'the Brusilov offensive', after the general who led it. But following some delusory early gains, the advance petered out. When the Germans and Austrians put in a counterstroke, the Russian army, its discipline and loyalty destroyed by the system of 'soldiers' councils', its men wishing simply to go home, melted away in a mob.

Yet in this same month of July, Kerensky succeeded in putting down a fresh popular rising in the streets of Petrograd – a rising that the Communist leaders themselves regarded as premature. With Lenin sheltering in exile in Helsinki, and his colleague Lev Trotsky in jail, it seemed as if Kerensky's parliamentary regime might yet survive. On 27 September Russia was officially proclaimed a republic, and on 20 October a preliminary parliament met in Petrograd to discuss Russia's future constitution. In an attempt at reconciliation, Trotsky and other Communist leaders were released.

In the aftermath of the German capture of Riga, however, rumours circulated that Kerensky's government was proposing to hand over the Russian capital, now ruled by a Communist soviet, to German occupation. On 26 October the Petrograd Soviet created a Military Revolutionary Committee under Trotsky; on 3 November the garrison acknowledged its authority. Trotsky, a brilliant organizer and tactician, now prepared a *coup d'état* with minute thoroughness. On 7 November (25 October by the old Russian calender then in use), when the Congress of Soviets from all over Russia was meeting in Petrograd, Trotsky's forces took over the city – telephone exchanges, post offices, railway stations and bridges. The provisional government in the Winter Palace possessed no armed forces capable of resisting the soldiers under Trotsky's command. It capitulated after a few persuasive shells from the Communist crew of the cruiser *Aurora* (preserved to this day as a monument), and Kerensky himself fled. Such was the successful *coup d'état* that Communists have celebrated ever since as 'the October Revolution'.

It remained only for the Communists to rivet their minority dictatorship on the Russian people. However, although the

Congress of Soviets gave executive power to a Committee of Commissars under Lenin, there came a setback in November, for in the elections to a constituent assembly, a large majority of Social Revolutionaries (or Democratic Socialists) was returned. Lenin nevertheless found an answer to this inconvenient development. When the constituent assembly met in Petrograd in January 1918, he dissolved it by force and arrested prominent anti-Communist members.

So Russia, a nation of 180,000,000 people, fell under a Communist government, perhaps for ever. Out of the havoc of 1917 had sprung the most fateful development in the history of the twentieth century.

At the time the warring nations were only conscious that a great ally and a great enemy had disappeared from the board, with all the consequences for the strategic balance. In December the Communist leadership signed an armistice with Germany and Austria at Brest-Litovsk.

TWELVE

The impact of total war

AS 1918 CAME IN, the Western Front remained, a ragged wound carved across the face of France and Belgium, the central fact of the war. To upset the equilibrium of power expressed by it, the belligerent nations were staking all their resources in the greatest collective effort ever generated by the human race. The Western Front itself presented a strange paradox. The opposing armies were mass organizations on a scale never seen before – apart from the field formations themselves, there were immense engineering workshops, supply depots, bakeries, general hospitals, veterinary hospitals and vast training camps like the notorious British 'Bull Ring' at Etaples. Yet the fighting itself at the point of contact on the battlefield was, by contrast, an affair of small isolated bodies of men – a section of half a dozen men or a machine-gun crew – struggling with similar enemy groups for possession of a segment of trench, a bunker or a shellhole.

Amid the crushing noise and violence of a great battle, the infantryman lived with a constant fear that surged at times into throat-choking terror. All about him lay the rotting evidence of how vulnerable was the human body to the high-velocity bullet and the jagged piece of flying shrapnel. Lucky were the instantaneously dead or those with the right kind of 'Blighty' – a wound severe enough to have the victim shipped home to 'Blighty' (slang for Britain), but not involving the loss of half a face or both legs, or a mangling of the bowels that left the patient functioning by means of some ghastly surgical makeshift. The bravest, staunchest man could endure battle for only a limited time. Then psychological exhaustion beyond tiredness or fear, beyond words, beyond sleep, sometimes beyond cure, took over.

Even on quiet sectors of the front, men lived daily with death and mutilation from the sniper's bullet, the routine salvo of shells, the machine-gun fire ripping across no-man's-land. Otherwise life on the Western Front was a matter of tedious routine, of fatigues and discomfort. Middle-class war writers were later to paint a dismal picture of existence in the trenches: the rats in the stinking dug-outs, the pole latrines, the lice in the sweat-stale clothing, the squalid ruination of the whole trench zone. All of it offered a painful enough contrast to the sheltered and comfortable existences enjoyed by these writers before the war. Yet to the majority of soldiers, being peasants or farm labourers or industrial workers from city slums, actual living conditions in and behind the line on quiet sectors were little if any worse than in peacetime. Certainly many British working-class soldiers enjoyed a better diet, better medical care and better welfare than they had as civilians.

Wartime diaries show how quickly the dangers of a routine tour in the line on a quiet sector could be shrugged off in favour of enjoyment of 'a good feed' of egg and chips in the canteen, a sing-song, a concert party or a film show.

Since it was the Western Front that barred the way of both sides to a victorious peace, much deep thought was devoted to devising a technological key to unlock it. Here was an unprece-dented military conundrum: a 400-mile front continuously and densely manned, plentifully equipped with firepower; the com-bined fruits of conscription, the huge increase of European popu-lation during the previous hundred years, and the industrial revolution. The heart of the problem lay in the lopsided state of military technology, for immensely destructive firepower was coupled with inflexibility and poor mobility.

While a complex telephone network admirably suited the needs of the static front and the base areas in the rear, it was inadequate as a means of communication and control during an offensive because shellfire again and again cut the lines run out across no-man's-land behind the advance. Morse-code wireless sets, heavy and cumbersome, provided only a limited answer. Only with the coming of walkie-talkies in the Second World War would commanders once more enjoy direct contact with their fighting units, as did Marlborough and Wellington. Again and again on the Western Front attacking troops passed out of their commanders' control beyond a gulf of silence or misinformation.

Railways and horse-drawn supply from fixed rail-heads like-wise suited the static front, but could not make possible a deep, fast-moving advance, least of all one beginning in the cratered mire of a battlefield. Even though motor transport made great progress during the war – in the case of the British army, from 827 cars and 15 motor cycles in 1914 to 56,000 trucks and 34,000 motor cycles in 1918 – the motor industries of the time simply could not produce enough vehicles to motorize mass armies. In any case, the vehicles themselves, clumsy, unreliable and solid-tyred, could not traverse a battlefield.

•

IT WAS IN THE VERY NATURE of a Great War battlefield that there lay the heart of the conundrum. The defence was so strong that only massed artillery could blast a path through it for the infantry. Yet it was this same artillery that created the wilderness that impeded all forward movement. As a result, advances were necessarily so slow and deliberate that the enemy always had time to bring up reserves and seal off an initial breach.

The ingenuity of the scientist and the engineer therefore sought some alternative to high explosive as a means of overcoming the defence. Germany, with her superb chemical industry, had turned to gas. In 1917 she introduced mustard gas fired in shells; one part of it to four million parts of air was sufficient to blister the human skin. By drenching a sector with gas shell in a short surprise bombardment (as at Riga), the attackers could neutralize the defenders without smashing up the ground. The British and French, though they did not neglect gas, strove to develop the tank, first used on the Somme in 1916 and again in Nivelle's offensive, for it promised to combine mobility with firepower and armoured protection. But it was not until November 1917 that

British industry produced enough tanks to make possible the first real tank battle, at Cambrai in Picardy.

On 20 November, without even registering the guns on to their targets beforehand by preliminary shots, a barrage from 1,000 guns crashed on the forward defences of the Hindenburg Line and rolled on. Behind the barrage and under cover of 300 aircraft clanked 378 tanks in cooperation with eight infantry divisions. The surprise, aided by fog, was complete. The tanks crunched over the wire and trenches and advanced in a single day as far as the British army had in months on the Somme and at Ypres, reaching the German rear zone some three or four miles behind the front line. However, Cambrai proved a one-day miracle. Sixty-five tanks were lost to German fire, another 71 broke down, and 43 got stuck in ditches. The battle turned into the old familiar confused slogging match, until a swiftly organized and deadly German counterstroke to a flank wiped out the British gains. Whatever its promise for the future, the tank was as yet too slow, too vulnerable and far too unreliable to transform the nature of warfare.

Artillery therefore dominated the battlefield, inflicting far higher casualties than the machine gun. Gunnery evolved into an exact science. Targets were determined by aerial reconnaissance; the fall of shot corrected by observers in captive balloons. The gunners fired from the map after complicated calculations of the effect of wind and weather on the shells' flight path. A great preliminary bombardment was orchestrated according to the elaborate schedules of a fire plan. When the infantry began its assault, the guns switched to a creeping barrage: a curtain of fire advancing just ahead of the infantry. The climax of an artillery war was reached when, on 23 March 1918, three colossal German guns mounted on special railway wagons began to bombard Paris at a range of 75 miles. These guns were nicknamed 'Big Berthas' after the wife of Gustav von Bohlen, head of Krupps, their manufacturer.

For the first time in history technology lofted warfare into the air. In 1914 the Royal Flying Corps had numbered 63 aircraft; in 1918 the newly created Royal Air Force numbered 22,000. It was a measure of the vast stride taken by airpower in four years.

Yet it still remained an adjunct of armies and navies rather than a decisive instrument of war in its own right, its tasks reconnaissance, aerial photography and 'strafing' the enemy's defences and nearby supply depots. In order to shield activities on the ground from prying eyes in the air, the art of camouflage was invented. Guns and other installations disappeared under netting coloured to merge with foliage.

It was not the workaday functions of the air forces that caught the public imagination but the exploits of the fighter aces. The task of the fighter squadrons lay in shooting down enemy observation balloons, artillery-spotting aircraft and bombers – and protecting those of their own side. This led to freewheeling 'dogfights' over the front between the opposing fighter forces. In a war of anonymous masses, the young fighter aces revived in modern form the individuality, gallantry and chivalry of combat in the past. France had her Georges Guynemer, with 54 kills to his credit; Britain's Albert Ball vc shot down 44 German aircraft before his own death, while Edward Mannock's score mounted to 73. Long before the United States entered the war in 1917, American pilots were fighting on the Western Front as volunteers in the 'Escadrille Lafayette'. The Escadrille was founded on 16 April 1916 and won fame over the battlefield of Verdun. By an irony, when the squadron was wound up in February 1918, all its members were pronounced medically unfit to join the new American Army Air Corps. Captain Eddie Rickenbacker, with 26 kills, became the Air Corps' outstanding flyer. Perhaps the most renowned of all the aces was the German Baron Manfred von Richthofen, 'the Red Baron', whose 'circus' of scarlet-painted Fokker triplanes became the most feared sights for Allied airmen. When he was finally shot down on 21 April 1918 after destroying 70 Allied aircraft, the Royal Air Force buried him with full military honours.

Airpower carried the war to enemy cities. At the end of 1916 Germany turned to long-range bombers because the vulnerable Zeppelin airships had been mastered by British fighters firing incendiary bullets. On 13 June 1917, 14 twin-engined Gothas, each carrying a one-ton bombload, took off on the first daylight raid on London, killing 162 people and injuring 432. In autumn 1917 the Gothas began to attack by night. Paris too was a target. By the end of the war there had been 52 enemy raids on Britain, in which 2,772 bombs were dropped, killing 857 people, injuring 2,058 and causing nearly £1,500,000 worth of damage. But the moral effects were out of all proportion to the material. The unexpected danger, the shattering noise of bombs and anti-aircraft guns, frayed the nerve of a population brought up in the safe tranquillity of Victorian and Edwardian England. War industry began to suffer because of absenteeism; at Woolwich Arsenal production fell to only a fifth of normal on the day after a raid.

British and French medium bomber forces struck from French bases at German targets in the Rhineland. In a single French raid on Karlsruhe in 1916 120 people were killed. But as a consequence of the Gotha heavy-bomber raids on southern England the British created the 'Independent Air Force' in June 1918, its purpose strategic bombing of the German homeland. Unfortunately production difficulties with its big, twin-engined heavy bombers meant that the force achieved relatively little before the end of the war. Yet from this tentative beginning was to grow the Bomber Command of the Second World War and the devastating strategic air offensive against Nazi Germany.

The dead or maimed civilians and the wrecked homes left by the bomber or the 'Big Bertha' gun appallingly demonstrated a general lesson – that there were no non-combatants in a total war. And, indeed, everybody had now been drawn in; everyone was doing his bit. As the battlefields swallowed up the men, the women had more and more taken over jobs at home. In Britain, for instance, the number of women in public transport rose 14 times between 1914 and 1918; doubled in commerce; rose by nearly a third in industry. For the first time women donned police uniform and joined the armed services. The WAACs (Women's Army Auxiliary Corps) served as cooks, typists, drivers and telephonists. The Wrens (Women's Royal Naval Service) acted as signallers, made mine nets, did maintenance work on torpedoes and depth charges. The WRAFs (Women's Royal Air Force) were employed as drivers and fitters. Women farm workers too put on uniform and became the Women's Land Army, for the world of total war was a world of uniforms, where even a cowshed became a kind of military post. War service won for British women the prize that had eluded the pre-war suffragettes. In Britain the Representation of the People Act of 1918 gave the vote to women over 30, together with the right to stand for Parliament, that ancient bastion of male privilege.

By now, all belligerent countries had come to practise 'war socialism' – state control and direction of almost every aspect of life. In Britain the Defence of the Realm Act ('Dora') gave the government virtually unlimited powers; in Germany the Auxiliary Service Law subjected all adults to conscription either for the armed forces or vital industry. It was through rationing that state control impinged most heavily on the life of the individual. Even Britain, with her strong free-trade and free-market Liberal tradition, finally introduced ration books at the beginning of 1918. The ration coupon became a second currency that even the better-off had to eke out with thrift. But British rations were lavish compared with German and Austrian. The Allied blockade, coupled with a shortage of labour and fertilizer on the farms and the gradual breakdown of transportation, had brought central Europe to the edge of outright starvation. A German doctor wrote of the children in his care: 'Thin and pale as corpses, they shoot up, mere skin and bone.'

Not only food, but every commodity was desperately short in Germany now, from lubricants to bandages and drugs. Europe's most dynamic industrial power found herself reduced to the level of a poor and backward country. Few private vehicles remained; public transport had almost stopped; trains travelled at only 20 miles per hour because of delapidated track and worn-out engines. The once mighty German economy was inexorably running down towards collapse, thanks to the Allied blockade but even more to the 'Hindenburg Programme' of 1916, which had sacrificed Germany's future existence to a short-term boost in munitions production.

With privation and grief the lot of all the warring nations, it was little wonder that 1917 saw further attempts to bring about a compromise peace. In the spring the new Austrian Emperor Karl (who succeeded to the throne on Franz Josef's death in December 1916) made secret approaches to the Allies, knowing that only an early peace could save his empire from disintegration. But it came to nothing: Karl could not commit his German ally, while Italy, bribed into the war by Allied promises of specific Austrian lands, would not settle for less even for the sake of enticing Austria to desert Germany. In June the Socialist International held a 'peace' conference in Stockholm to which delegates from belligerent and neutral countries were invited. The German government permitted their nationals to attend; the British and French governments did not. In July the German Reichstag actually passed a 'peace resolution', but in such studiously vague terms as to render it meaningless. In August the Vatican addressed a peace note to the belligerents, without result. In November Lord Lansdowne wrote a letter to *The Times* repeating the doubts he had expressed privately to the Cabinet a year before, but succeeded only in drawing on himself indignant popular outcry. And in all countries sporadic strikes and street demonstrations continued.

The available evidence goes to show that the majority in every belligerent country still remained stubbornly resolved to stick it out. They felt that the very sacrifices made since 1914 must be redeemed by a victorious peace. Like two sides of a family split by a quarrel, each side was more than ever convinced that it was in the right and the enemy was totally in the wrong. The press continued to nourish this entrenched hatred. Elaborate government propaganda machines, surely among the most repellent of the developments brought about by total war, worked to rot the will of the enemy peoples and stiffen that of their own. Atrocity stories, such as the one about German 'corpse factories' for making soap out of the dead, were started on their rounds. The new medium of the cinema was pressed into service along with the poster and printed word.

In Britain, Germany and France the people continued to believe that strong leaders would pull them through; and as long as they could still hope, they would fight on. In August 1917 Hindenburg, Ludendorff and GHQ finally won supreme power in Germany when their tame nominee, Georg Michaelis, became Chancellor in place of Bethmann-Hollweg. In France the advent of Georges Clemenceau to the premiership in November, as ferocious a patriot as he was a man, signalled the ruthless crushing of defeatist and pacifist elements. 'Home policy? I wage war! Foreign policy? I wage war! All the time I wage war!' The faith of the Allied nations in the righteousness of their cause was strengthened by the final Treaty of Brest-Litovsk between Germany and Communist Russia on 3 March 1918, which showed just what peace on Germany's terms could mean. For Russia had to cede a third of her population, half her industry and nine-tenths of her coal mines.

Below Parisians queuing for coal. Commodities all over Europe were in short supply. **Bottom** British soldiers behind a wire barrier on a road at St-Jean during the Battle of the Lys, April 1918. **Overleaf** German prisoners captured during the second Battle of the Somme near Amiens, August 1918 – a brilliant British success.

Opposite top British tanks rapidly fell victim to breakdowns and German gunfire. This photograph shows one of the surviving Mark IV tanks on the Amiens Road on 10 August 1918. **Opposite bottom** Eleftherios Venizelos, the Greek prime minister, being greeted by officers of the Allied forces on his arrival at Salonika in October 1916. **Below** Bulgarians making a last stand on the heights of Monastir during the Balkan campaign. The French captured the town in November 1916.

Below Allied troops entering Baghdad, 'City of the Caliphs', on 11 March 1917 after overcoming Turkish resistance. **Opposite top** The British breakthrough of the formidable Hindenburg Line – bringing ammunition supplies across the dried-up Canal du Nord on 27 September 1918. **Opposite below** On 11 November 1918 the German armistice delegation met Allied representatives led by Ferdinand Foch (front row, second from the right) in a restaurant car on a railway siding in the Forest of Compiègne.

Below America announces the end of the war and New York celebrates.

To Hindenburg and Ludendorff, however, the elimination of Russia and the Eastern Front, an accomplished fact since the armistice at Brest-Litovsk the previous November, signified Germany's last chance to win the war by defeating Britain and France on the Western Front before the Americans arrived in overwhelming force.

THIRTEEN
The emperor's battle

ON 11 NOVEMBER 1917 a conference took place in Mons to decide Germany's national strategy for 1918. No civilian frock-coats were present, not even the Chancellor; only the field-grey uniforms and carmine collar flashes of generals and the general staff. It was a sign of how completely German destiny had fallen into the hands of the military. Ludendorff, who presided, came to the meeting with his mind already made up in favour of staking Germany's last reserves of strength on a grand spring offensive on the Western Front. He saw no alternative. Germany's failing economy and shaky home front ruled out a prolonged defensive struggle. So too did the condition of her allies, Austria, Bulgaria and Turkey. The German army itself, the central engine of the whole war, 'thought with horror of fresh defensive battles', wrote Ludendorff, 'and longed for a war of movement'. To Ludendorff therefore everything pointed to 'an offensive that would bring about an early decision. This was only possible on the Western Front.'

The Mons conference began more than two months of argument as to what form this offensive should take. One school favoured a double attack on both sides of Verdun, so bringing about a wide collapse in the French Front. Ludendorff himself decided in favour of attacking the British. Two main proposals emerged: 'Michael', an offensive between Arras and Saint-Quentin northwestwards to the Channel coast, and 'George', a more modest operation across the River Lys in Flanders towards the key British communications centre of Hazebrouck, which would take in flank and rear the British forces and base installations crammed between Ypres and the sea. Typically, Ludendorff settled in the end for 'Michael', even though able staff officers argued that it was beyond Germany's strength. 'If this blow succeeded,' wrote Ludendorff later, 'the strategic result might indeed be enormous, as we should separate the bulk of the English army from the French and crowd it up with its back to the sea.' Thus Imperial Germany in 1918, as in 1914, staked her future on a grandiose military gamble.

Throughout the winter of 1917–18 troops were sent by rail from the virtually defunct Eastern Front and, together with selected units withdrawn from the Western Front, trained in new offensive tactics. Instead of fixed linear objectives, there was to be rapid infiltration through the enemy defence by storm groups of infantry, machine guns and field artillery. Reserves were to be fed in where the attack was progressing rather than where it was held up. The storm groups were to flow forward by paths of least resistance, like a tide coming in over a rocky foreshore.

As February turned to March, no fewer than 47 special attack divisions and over 6,000 guns were deployed with all their stores and transport behind a front already manned by 28 trench divisions, all with utmost secrecy.

Despite the German measures of concealment Allied intelligence plotted the build-up of German strength in the West with remarkable accuracy. Although the Allies realized what a hurricane was brewing, they failed to take adequate measures to meet it. Even after three and a half years of war there was still no unified Allied command on the Western Front. Largely at Lloyd George's urging, an inter-Allied Supreme War Council had been set up, composed of statesmen and soldiers, to coordinate Allied strategy on all fronts. The British War Premier attempted to enhance its authority over the national commanders-in-chief via a military committee chaired by General Ferdinand Foch (French Chief of Staff and France's military representative on the War Council), which would control an Anglo-French central reserve. On paper a reasonable idea, it really marked another devious attempt by Lloyd George to bypass Haig and Robertson. Robertson resigned rather than accept that Lloyd George would no longer take military advice from him, but from the British military representative on the Supreme War Council, General Sir Henry Wilson, a glib, charming but unsound soldier whom the politicians liked. Haig and Pétain (who, for his part, deeply mistrusted Foch) sabotaged the proposed central reserve by stating that they could spare no troops for it. Thus smouldering suspicions and rivalries continued to bedevil Allied planning. In the end Haig and Pétain each planned his own defensive battle, with limited arrangements for mutual help on either side of the junction of their two armies.

Haig, Ludendorff's intended victim, was three per cent weaker in fighting strength than a year before, even though he had taken over an extra 28 miles of front from the French. Although he had asked the War Cabinet for fresh drafts of 600,000 men, the Cabinet, in order to curb his wish to take the offensive, had released only 100,000. He was also instructed to reorganize his divisions into nine battalions each instead of 12, radical and unsettling surgery only completed on the eve of the German attack.

In deploying his available strength, Haig was particularly concerned with his left flank in Flanders, where even a short German advance could imperil all the communications and base installations between the Ypres front and the Channel – the very 'George' plan that Ludendorff had discarded. Haig judged that on his right flank on the Somme he had room behind the front to give ground before a German advance while reserves came up to the rescue. Despite ever firmer evidence that the German blow was in fact going to fall on his right-flank armies, the Third and Fifth, Haig however allotted them only two-thirds the strength in proportion to front that he did to his left-flank armies in Flanders. The Fifth Army, next to the French, was particularly weak, with only 12 infantry divisions to 42 miles of front, the bulk of them tired and shaken survivors of Third Ypres.

Although in the short time available the weary soldiers dug and dug as well as trained, the defence system on the Fifth Army front was still unfinished when the enemy struck; the main battle

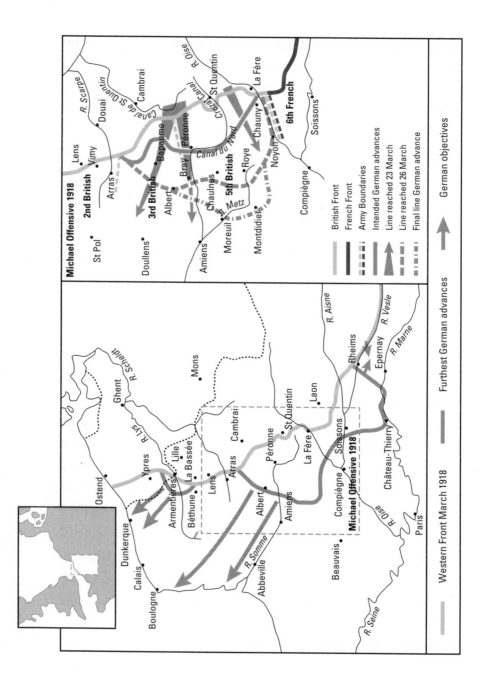

zone was devoid of all dug-outs and the rear zone just a line of turned turf. Instead of offering a defence in depth, a third of the Fifth Army's strength was packed into the completed forward zone – ready victims for the German bombardment and first assault.

On 18 March, three days before the launch date of the 'Michael' offensive, Allied intelligence calculated that the German army in the west was 37 divisions stronger than in November 1917. Yet to counter-balance this vast increase in strength there was at present only a single American division in the line, plus three in training – and this more than a year after the United States had entered the war.

•

AMERICA HAD FACED UNIQUE PROBLEMS in creating a mass army. Her peacetime army had been even smaller than that of the British. Whereas before the war the British had at least formed an expeditionary force and drawn up blueprints for staff methods and field formations, the Americans in 1917 had to start from scratch in every way – even having to decide the size, organization and equipment of the basic infantry division. At least America learned from her own dismal experience of voluntary recruiting during the Civil War and adopted conscription ('the Draft') straight away. Huge training camps had to be built and staffed: factories for mass-producing 'doughboys' much as Henry Ford turned out Model Ts. More vast camps had to be constructed

Opposite: **The Geman Offensive, March–July 1918.**

along the eastern seaboard to accommodate troops awaiting shipment across the Atlantic. Shortage of shipping constituted a major bottleneck in the flow of America's young strength to Europe.

General Pershing, the Commander-in-Chief of the American Expeditionary Force, had resolved to build up an independent, self-contained American army rather than see his troops fed piecemeal into British or French formations. This policy, though understandable, meant further delay before American soldiers reached the line, while complete divisions, with their headquarters, artillery and supply services, were organized.

It would therefore be the battle-stained, under-strength British and French who would bear the brunt of the coming supreme crisis of the war.

•

ON 16 MARCH the 47 attack divisions of the 'Michael' offensive began marching the last stages to their launch positions. Elated by the vast scale of the preparations, the troops sang their way along in eagerness and optimism. In truth, the last of Germany's strength had gone into contracting a muscle that could strike one great blow and no more. Even the 'Michael' divisions desperately lacked horses, and shortages of petrol, oil and rubber crippled motor transport. Manpower reserves were down to 18-year-olds and younger. Nor could the German home front survive more tribulations, as demonstrated by a mass strike in January in Berlin and other cities, demanding peace with no annexations and no indemnities – a slogan borrowed from the Russian Communists.

Suffering and loss had by now corroded away to a thin crust the
national unity forged by patriotic emotion in 1914.

By 19 March Hindenburg, Ludendorff and the Kaiser had
all arrived at advanced headquarters in Avesnes, ready for the
launching on 21 March of what had now been flatteringly dubbed
the *Kaiserschlacht* – the 'emperor's battle'.

The British on the Third and Fifth Army fronts knew the
offensive was imminent from cumulative intelligence reports. The
evening of 20 March was quiet. By 9 p.m. a mist had begun to
thicken into fog, damping sound, isolating each post.
Apprehension prickled along the silent line. In the small hours the
fog thickened further.

On the stroke of 4.40 a.m. (German time) on 21 March 1918
6,000 German guns crashed out together. For five stunning hours
the subtly orchestrated bombardment beat on the whole depth of
the British defence system: high explosive against buried telephone lines and guns, headquarters and telephone exchanges;
phosgene and mustard gas against fighting troops. The bombardment reduced the Fifth Army, and to some extent the Third, to
isolated and uncoordinated elements of gassed and blasted troops.
The sun rose at 6 a.m., but the fog still lay thick along low
ground, blinding the defence. At 9.40 a.m. the German guns
switched to a creeping barrage, and the storm groups swiftly
followed. This was the moment when the spell of paralysis that
had been laid on the Western Front in 1914 began to be lifted.

On the front of attack, from north of Cambrai to south of
Saint-Quentin, the three 'Michael' armies enjoyed an overwhelming
superiority of men and firepower – especially on the over-extended

Fifth Army front. The forward zone of defence was swamped in an hour or so. By midday the Fifth Army had lost a third of its strength; by mid-afternoon the German storm groups were driving deep into the British battle zone. By nightfall, on the Fifth Army front south of the Somme, the attackers had penetrated beyond the British gun line into open country; a true break-through at last.

A disaster in itself for the British, 21 March presaged even greater dangers as the Fifth Army and a part of the Third began to fall back in confusion with the German attack divisions at their heels. The long-fixed organizations of a static front – army, corps headquarters and heavy artillery – began to pack up in haste and take to crowded roads. Already Haig was switching reserves from Flanders to his disintegrating right flank; Pétain dispatched seven French divisions instead of the three requested that day by the British Commander-in-Chief. By 23 March the Fifth Army's defence had foundered into headlong retreat; the bridgehead of Péronne was lost; a gap opened between the Fifth and the Third Armies. Only the remnants of the Fifth Army stretched along 40 miles of front stood between the Germans and the key rail centre of Amiens. If the Germans could take Amiens, the British and French armies would be driven apart, so leading to total catastrophe. Haig therefore appealed to Pétain to concentrate 20 French divisions in the Amiens area. Pétain, fearing a second German blow against his own front in Champagne, refused, but did offer to take over the Fifth Army front as far north as Péronne.

The 'March Retreat' was now in full swing:

Agitated staff officers galloped wildly across country, vainly searching for troops for whom they had orders but could not find. Roads and villages were packed with transport and units on the move; everywhere those who had been 'pushed off' the roads made their way...to the accompaniment of the rattle of machine-gun and rifle fire and shell bursts; flames from burning stores, canteens and hutments threw such a glare over the old Somme battlefields as to illumine the darkness and provide light by which all could see.

On 23 March, therefore, Ludendorff was presented with the opportunity of transforming his brilliant initial success into the decisive victory he craved. He muffed it by giving his three 'Michael' armies divergent axes of advance instead of concentrating everything on reaching Amiens. Thus dispersed, the German effort was to weaken day by day. In any case boots and hooves and scarce iron-tyred lorries could not maintain the momentum of the offensive as the German tanks and motor transport were to do in 1940.

Yet to the Allied command the danger still seemed to be growing. On 24 March Haig learned to his horror that Pétain, in his concern for covering Paris, was prepared to allow the French army to become separated from the British. Two days later, at Haig's urgent instigation, a conference of Allied statesmen and soldiers under President Poincaré was held in the little town of Doullens. This conference resulted in the appointment of Foch as Allied Supreme Commander on the Western Front. Nevertheless, whatever the moral effect of appointing the fiery-spirited Foch above the defeatist Pétain, it made little difference to the actual course of the battle. The crisis had already begun to pass. While Allied reserves flowed to the defence of Amiens, the German effort steadily faded and the German advance slowed and slowed. For the attacking troops were sagging with fatigue and exhaustion, harrassed by massed Allied air attack, and distracted by plunder of British stores and canteens.

On 28 March Ludendorff launched a fresh attack against the Arras sector, only to see it repulsed with heavy loss. Too late he now gave the 'Michael' forces the single objective of Amiens. By the beginning of April his troops had marched and fought to a standstill, while the Allies had consolidated a new front covering the town. On 4–5 April the Germans made a last effort to reach Amiens, but were stopped 10 miles short of it. 'Michael', the 'emperor's battle', was over. The Germans had advanced 28 miles and taken 70,000 prisoners – a brilliant battlefield performance that nevertheless had ended in a gigantic strategic failure.

Now Ludendorff had to try again elsewhere, even though 'Michael' had consumed 250,000 men out of his precious man-power reserves. On 9 April he struck in Flanders across the Lys – the original Operation 'George', now emasculated into 'Georgette'. A Portuguese division gave way and the Germans thrust on towards Hazebrouck. By the 11th they were within miles of this key rail centre, and Haig issued an Order of the Day: 'There must be no retirement. With our backs to the wall and believing in the justice of our cause each one must fight on to the end.' They fought on, a resolute, well-conducted defence that by 18 April wore the Germans to a standstill.

The failure to smash the British forced Ludendorff to rethink his entire strategy. Since 21 March he had lost nearly 350,000 men and inflicted similar losses. During that period nearly 180,000 more American troops had arrived in France; three US divisions (equal in strength to six European divisions) were already in the Allied line. Although Germany's margin of strength and time was fast running out, Ludendorff decided to take further gambles: attacks on the French Front to draw back the French reserves that had gone to Haig's support, and then a final victorious offensive against the weakened British in Flanders.

On 27 May he struck on the Chemin des Dames with 30 attack divisions (only 15 of them fresh), engulfing a defence foolishly deployed too far forward. The German spearheads swept over the Aisne and on to the south. By the 30th they were on the Marne, only 37 miles from Paris. In the Second Battle of the Marne the German advance faltered and died against new French defence positions strong in artillery. There was an ominous novelty in this fresh setback: on 6 July the 2nd United States Division recaptured Belleau Wood, near Château-Thierry, its buoyant dash making up for want of skill and experience. Already on 28 May the 1st US Division had seen action on the Somme, capturing the village of Cantigny.

On 9 June Ludendorff attacked again between Noyons and Montdidier, but with only local success. While German reserves were melting away, Ludendorff estimated that 15 US Divisions reached France between April and the end of June. Still he clung to the hope of smashing the British before the balance of strength swung fatally against him. On 15 July he launched a final preliminary onslaught against the French, this time on either side of Reims. To the west of the city the Germans established a bridgehead across the Marne; but to the east their attack broke down completely in the face of a French defence in depth.

Nonetheless, Ludendorff believed that the time was now ripe to prepare the final blow against the British in Flanders, code-named 'Hagen'. On 18 July, in the middle of a staff conference on 'Hagen', came the stunning news that the French had launched a massive surprise counterstroke against the west flank of the German salient on the Marne. 'Hagen' was dead; the whole supreme German effort for 1918 had failed.

FOURTEEN

The black day of the German army

COMING AFTER THE YARD-BY-YARD, month-by-month Allied advances of 1916–17, the sudden German breakthroughs of spring 1918 towards the Channel ports and Paris had shocked and alarmed the Allied nations and their leaders. Yet the German successes had at no point come near to fulfilling Ludendorff's intention 'to shake the position of Lloyd George and Clemenceau' and 'make the enemy inclined to peace'. The British War Cabinet, whose refusal to provide Haig with his requested reinforcements had contributed to the disaster of 21 March, now poured troops into France. Clemenceau (all too aptly nicknamed 'the Tiger') and Foch thought of nothing but exacting a bloody revenge for Germany's fresh conquests. America, abruptly realizing that her allies might not be able to hold on very much longer, spurred the deployment of her own strength.

On 28 March General Pershing temporarily abandoned his

policy of creating an independent American army and offered his hard-pressed allies all the troops he had, to use as they needed. This was how the 1st US Division came to fight at Cantigny on the Somme on 28 May under British corps and army command, and the 2nd and 3rd Divisions under French command along the Marne in June and July.

Here was welcome succour at a desperate period. But far more important for the issue of the war was a new policy adopted by the United States for shipping American troops across the Atlantic. Instead of transporting complete divisions with all their space-hungry guns and equipment, soldiers alone would be sent. The divisions would be formed and equipped in France – with British and French material. This not only made immense savings in shipping space, but also overcame the bottleneck caused by desperately slow American production of new and untried designs of weapons. Whereas in 1915–16 American industry had saved the Allies from defeat by supplying munitions, steel and machine tools, now Britain and France in their turn were to arm the American Expeditionary Force: Britain with its heavy artillery, trench mortars and steel helmets; France with its medium and field artillery and its aircraft.

Under the impact of the German spring offensives, therefore, the flow of strength across the Atlantic swelled quickly into a mighty flood. In March only 84,000 Americans had arrived in France; in May 246,000; in July 306,703 – nearly half of them in British vessels, made available by Britain cutting down her imports. These figures, immensely higher than the German High Command had thought possible, spelled defeat for Germany.

Her own losses in the spring offensives, coming on top of her enormous casualties in the attrition battles of 1916 and 1917, had consumed the last of her manpower reserves. All that remained were 300,000 youths of the 1919 class called up in June. A German battalion now on average numbered only 660 men instead of about 900 at the end of 1917. Thanks to the very German advances in the spring offensives, this depleted army held a far longer and weaker front than in March – temporary defences instead of formidable systems like the Hindenburg Line.

In the middle of July, therefore, the campaign of 1918 came quivering to a balance. Foch, like Joffre at the Marne in September 1914, divined that the moment was ripe to go over to the offensive. Using the lush green cover of the Forest of Villers-Cotterêts to conceal his assembly, Foch resolved to smash in the western flank of the German salient, which hung like a sack down to the Marne. General Charles Mangin, Commander of the Tenth Army, France's most ruthless fighting soldier, was put in charge of the operation, for which he was allotted 24 divisions (four of them American), over 2,000 guns and 900 aircraft. The French army's Moroccan Division and the US 1st and 2nd Divisions would deliver the opening punch: a formidable combination, for the Moroccans and Senegalese under their French officers were crack troops, while the Americans were all regular soldiers. This time there was to be no preliminary bombardment at all, but a creeping barrage with the infantry and 400 French tanks coming on behind like a sudden avalanche.

At 4.35 a.m. on 18 July the pendulum of war began finally to swing against Germany. According to an American eyewitness:

Miles of close-laid batteries opened with one stupendous thunder. The air above the tree-tops spoke with unearthly noises, the shriek and rumble of light and heavy shells. Forward through the woods, very near, rose up a continued crashing war of explosions, and a murk of smoke, and a hell of bright fires continually renewed. It only lasted five minutes, that barrage... But they were terrible minutes for the unsuspecting Boche. Dazed, beaten down, and swept away, he tumbled out of his holes when it lifted, only to find the long bayonets of the Americans licking like flame across his forward positions, and those black devils, the Senegalese, raging with knives in his rifle pits.

The German line, weakly held, gave way; by noon Mangin's troops had advanced four miles through the standing corn. Next day, after a dispute between the cautious Pétain and the ardent Foch and Mangin, the attack continued, winning another two miles of ground. The bag of prisoners rose to 15,000; of guns to 400. The Americans had also now learned the cruel price of battle on the Western Front: in two days the 2nd Division alone lost 5,000 men.

On Ludendorff the impact of the Allied counterstroke was shattering. In his panic and rage he even quarrelled furiously with Hindenburg. On the morning of 19 July a colleague found him 'in a really agitated and nervous state' – in fact, one of mental paralysis. It was the continuing Allied offensive north of the Marne, in which four British and two Italian divisions now joined, that made up his mind for him; he ordered his troops to fall back from the Marne to the River Vesle. Hindenburg's memoirs sum up the catastrophic results for Germany of the Allied counterstroke:

> From the purely military point of view it was of the greatest and most fateful importance that we had lost the initiative to the enemy...
>
> The effect of our failure on the country and our allies was even greater, judging by first impressions.
>
> How many hopes, cherished during the last few months, had probably collapsed at one blow! How many calculations had been scattered to the winds.

Although the immediate military crisis passed when the German troops dug in along the Vesle, Ludendorff's own mental crisis still burned on, to the deep anxiety of his colleagues, for he displayed total strategic indecision coupled with endless interfering in detail. By the beginning of August, however, he seemed to be recovering his balance. But on the 8th Sir Douglas Haig knocked him down mentally for good by launching a devastating surprise counterstroke on the Somme.

•

ALTHOUGH FOCH ENJOYED THE TITLE of Allied Commander-in-Chief, he possessed none of the powers vested in Dwight Eisenhower in the Second World War; nor was there an integrated Allied headquarters and command structure of the kind first created in 1942. Foch could operate only by persuading the

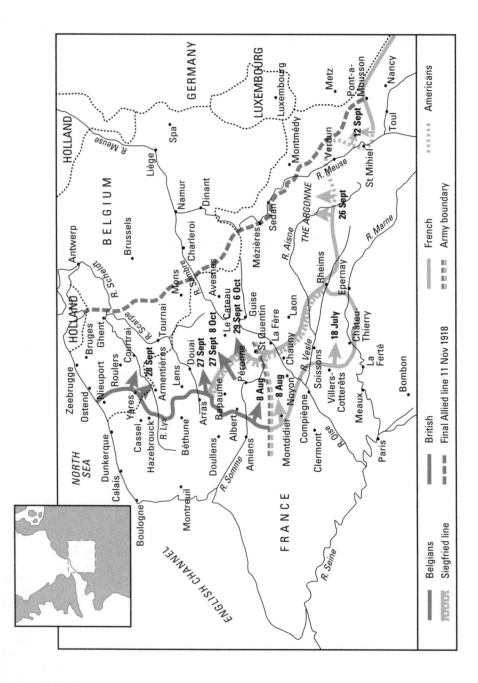

national commanders-in-chief to fall in with his plans. As it happened, it was Foch who more often than not was to fall in with Haig's ideas during the remainder of the 1918 campaign. At a conference at Foch's headquarters in the Château de Bombon on 24 July Foch agreed to Haig's proposal for an attack east of Amiens to clear the enemy further away from the vital Paris–Amiens–Calais railway. British intelligence knew that the German Front here was weak; in fact the defending German Second Army amounted to only seven battle-mauled divisions with two in reserve, each amounting to perhaps 3,000 rifles, holding defences that were hastily dug where the March offensive had finally expired.

Haig entrusted the offensive to the Fourth Army under General Sir Henry Rawlinson, the same general who had planned and conducted the First Battle of the Somme. Rawlinson, like his soldiers, had learned much since then, and the preparations for the coming Second Battle of the Somme made an astonishing contrast to those for the First. To help disguise the movement of the Canadian Corps from Flanders to the Somme, bogus radio traffic simulated Canadian headquarters in its old position. An apparent thinning of the British Front on the Somme convinced the German command that no attack was imminent. No troops were permitted to march *towards* the front during daylight hours. Allied fighters kept enemy reconnaissance aircraft at bay. Down to small details every aspect of the assembly of the attacking forces was characterized by concealment and deception.

Opposite: **The Allied Offensives, July–November 1918.**

The front of attack lay astride the Somme between the Ancre and the Avre, with the French First Army (assigned by Foch to Haig) occupying the third of it that lay south of the Amiens–Roye road. Rawlinson's own army comprised the Australian Corps and the Canadian Corps, which (with the New Zealanders) had emerged as the shock troops of Haig's command because of their aggression and initiative, and the British Third Corps and the Cavalry Corps: in all, 10 full-strength Dominion divisions, four British, one American and three cavalry – nearly 450,000 men. In the air the Allies outnumbered the enemy by five to one. This time there would be no ponderous fortnight-long preliminary bombardment, as in the First Battle of the Somme in 1916, but instead 342 heavy tanks and 72 of the new eight-miles-per-hour light Whippet tanks would smash through the enemy defences under cover of a creeping barrage of over 2,000 guns and howitzers.

The early morning of 8 August 1918, like that of 21 March, saw mist thickening along the front. The German Second Army, listless and dispirited after the failure of the March offensive, suspected nothing. At 4.20 a.m. (British time) the British guns dropped a curtain of fire and steel that began inexorably to move forward over the German positions. Behind the curtain came the tanks and infantry. As the tanks reared, loomed and lumbered through the shifting mist and smoke, the enemy collapsed in rout. All the scenes of confusion in the British line on 21 March were now replayed in German uniform.

By mid-morning the sun had warmed away the mist, and Allied airmen gazed down on Rawlinson's advancing army – a very different spectacle from the mud-bound attackers of 1916–17:

...the whole Santerre plateau...was dotted with parties of infantry, field artillery and tanks moving forward. Staff officers were galloping about, many riding horses in battle for the first time... Indeed, at this stage there was more noise of movement than firing, as the heavy batteries... were no longer in action.

The Whippet tanks ranged about the enemy's rear, even taking by surprise a corps staff at lunch, while Allied aircraft strafed all that moved: previews of the warfare of the future. In a final display of long traditional warfare, the cavalry (still in 1918 the fastest cross-country force) rounded up demoralized German infantry.

By the end of the day Rawlinson had advanced four miles, and, according to German accounts, virtually annihilated the defending divisions. Canadian and Australian losses barely exceeded 6,000.

'August 8,' wrote Ludendorff, 'was the black day of the German army in the history of this war.' The Second Battle of the Somme finally closed any last loophole of hope that the results of the French counterstroke of 18 July might not be final. Worse, it brought brutally home to Ludendorff that the morale and discipline of the German army were cracking at last:

...whole bodies of our men had surrendered to single troopers, or isolated squadrons. Retiring troops, meeting a fresh division going bravely into action, had shouted out things like 'Blackleg' and 'You're prolonging the war'... The officers in many places had lost their influence and allowed themselves to be swept along with the rest.

Fortunately for Ludendorff, Rawlinson's troops failed to exploit their initial success. The tanks quickly became a spent force, victims of breakdowns and German gunfire. On 9 August there were only 145 runners; on the 10th 85; on the 11th 38; and on the 12th just six. Whatever the future promise of the tank, the models of 1918 were simply not capable of sustained long-distance thrusts. The British command and communications system too, so long accustomed to the static front, fumbled the task of directing a fast-moving advance. As the British pressure relented, the German command found time and troops to patch up a new front.

The passing of the immediate emergency did not put an end to Ludendorff's nightmare. For in his own words, 'The 8th of August put the decline of [our] fighting power beyond all doubt, and in such a situation as regards reserves, I had no hope of finding a strategic expedient whereby to turn the situation to our advantage.' On 10 August he reported in this despairing vein to the Kaiser, who responded by observing: 'I see we must balance the books, we are at the limit of our powers. The War must be brought to an end.'

FIFTEEN

War against the Bulgar and the Turk

IT HAD TAKEN FOUR YEARS of gigantic and unrelenting effort to bring imperial Germany to this point of gasping weakness – at first in mass battles on both the Eastern Front and the Western Front, and since mid-1917 on the Western Front alone. Yet while this struggle with German might was in progress, nearly three million soldiers of the British Empire and large Allied contingents besides were drawn in turn into far-off sideshows with Germany's satellites.

By the summer of 1918 an Allied army had been sitting in northern Greece for three years, sucking in ever greater resources in manpower, material and shipping, the legacy of the soaring vision in spring 1915 of outflanking the Western Front by marching on Vienna via the Balkans. At the beginning of 1916, after the final failure at Gallipoli and the collapse of Serbia, the Allied Commander-in-Chief at Salonika, the French General Maurice

Sarrail, proceeded to construct an elaborate 70-mile-long defensive perimeter around the port, in order to hold it against an expected Bulgarian offensive coming out of the mountains to the north. The attack never came; the Allied bridgehead in technically neutral Greece became, in a derisive German phrase, 'the greatest internment camp in the world', already containing 90,000 British and 60,000 French troops. Italians came to join the throng; two Russian brigades as well. Here the remnants of the Serbian army rallied and prepared for their revenge.

In September 1916 the Allied forces at long last launched an offensive of their own, striking into the forbiddingly wild mountains between Greece and Serbia where the Bulgarians, with a stiffening of Germans, had dug themselves in with skill. Painfully the Allies drove the enemy from crest to crest as the mud of autumn gave way to the first blizzards of winter. Finally, in November, the French captured the town of Monastir, whereupon the Balkan campaign reverted to trance for the winter. Not until April and May 1917 did the Allies try again, attacking the series of steep and naked mountain ridges that extend along Greece's borders with Albania, Serbia and Bulgaria. The standard Great War tactical pattern repeated itself: breakdown of communications and control in the attacking forces; slaughter of troops in the open by emplaced guns and machine guns; small gains of ground. The Allied 'Army of the Orient', now at its peak strength of 600,000 men, reverted to the defensive again. In June 1917 the ever-deeper Allied involvement in Greece's internal affairs reached a climax with the enforced deposition of King Constantine in favour of his son, and the entry of Greece into the war under the

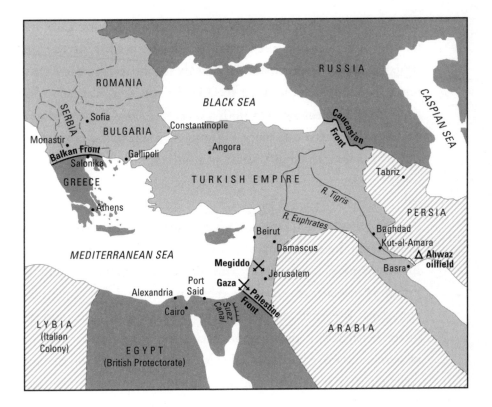

Above: **The Levant and the Middle East.**

pro-Allied Venizelos. Militarily, little further was to happen on the Greek Front for another 14 months. Malaria caused the bulk of Allied casualties. Men passed through the hospitals more than once, so that while a total of 409,000 British served at Salonika, the total of sick rose to 481,000, a ratio of 1,103 hospital admissions for sickness alone per 1,000 men – a staggering figure that underlines the campaign's waste and futility.

●

IN THE MIDDLE EAST, TOO, a major campaign had grown from small beginnings, eventually to swallow nearly 1,200,000 British Empire troops. In 1914 the Turkish Empire extended over the modern territories of Syria, the Lebanon, Jordan, Israel (Palestine) and down the Red Sea coast of modern Saudi Arabia. Turkish forces in Palestine therefore menaced the Suez Canal, Britain's imperial lifeline between the Mother Country and India, Australia and New Zealand, and Indian and Anzac units were dispatched to Egypt, a British protectorate, in order to defend the Canal. Early in 1915 the expected Turkish offensive materialized. Twenty thousand men marched through the heart of the Sinai Desert, where Egyptians and Israelis were to clash half a century later, and sought to cross the Canal. The defenders repulsed the Turks easily in what were hardly more than skirmishes.

Nonetheless, the British remained anxious lest the Turks should return in greater strength. They therefore dug a powerful defence system behind the Canal and built up the imperial garrison in Egypt to 100,000 by the end of 1915. Conscious of their new strength, the British cautiously pushed forward across the

Sinai. On 21 December 1916 El Arish, on the border of Palestine, fell. Lloyd George, who had just become War Premier, now saw a wonderful opportunity of winning a prize that would make better headlines in 1917 than another slog on the Western Front: the capture of Jerusalem, the Holy City of three religions. In January British imperial forces under General Sir Archibald Murray advanced into Palestine. On 24 March he attacked Gaza, garrisoned by 4,000 Turks. The plan was bold: a frontal infantry assault from the south, coupled with a cavalry sweep around the Turkish rear. The execution was muddled. By the time the infantry, after much confusion and loss, had fought its way into the city, the cavalry commander, believing the infantry had failed, had withdrawn his cordon from the Turkish rear. Turkish reinforcements poured in, and next day, amid more confusions, the British fell back.

Three weeks later Murray tried again, this time with a simple frontal attack by three infantry divisions against a ridge protecting Gaza from the south. This was a complete failure that cost Murray his command.

His successor, General Sir Edmund Allenby, lately commanding the Third Army on the Western Front, fully lived up to his nickname of 'the Bull' both in physique and character. A cavalryman, he now proceeded to make maximum use of his splendid Australian horsemen and of the opportunities for mobile warfare offered by the sweeping plains of southern Palestine. On 31 October he launched the Third Battle of Gaza. Carefully planted false information, together with a feint attack, convinced the enemy command that the main British effort would fall yet again on the coastal sector round Gaza. Instead Allenby seized Beersheba, the eastern hinge of the Turkish line, in a surprise attack, and sent his cavalry riding on for the sea across the Turkish rear. On 6 November a final blow at the Turkish centre, between Gaza and Beersheba, brought about the collapse of the enemy defence. Allenby's forces pushed on north through the cypress-sheltered orange groves to capture the ancient port of Jaffa, then swung east to climb the twisting road through the Judaean hills to Jerusalem on their crest. After fighting briefly on the rocky hillsides round the city, the Turks fell back northwards to Nablus. On 11 December 1917 Allenby entered Jerusalem, walking on foot, and Lloyd George had his desired Christmas present to cheer up the British people after a grim year. Nevertheless, Allenby's successes had by no means knocked Turkey out of the war, let alone inflicted damage on Germany. The campaign in Palestine had almost another year to run before it reached its final dead end.

•

THE SWITCH FROM COAL-BURNING to oil-burning ships had rendered British seapower dependent on supplies from the Persian oilfield at the head of the Persian Gulf. Yet less than 100 miles distant from the oil port of Abadan and the vital pipeline running inland to the wells round Ahwaz lay the borders of Turkish Mesopotamia (modern Iraq). On 6 November 1914, the day after Turkey's declaration of war, an infantry brigade group from India began to land near Basra, its mission to protect the Persian oilfields and pipeline. On 21 November Basra fell, and the

British pushed upstream to Al Qirnah on the Tigris. Another British force marched to the Persian town of Ahwaz and, after various skirmishes, eliminated the menace of raiding Turks and Arabs. In April 1915 a Turkish attempt to recapture Basra was beaten off.

The British had thus fully accomplished their original purpose. The government of India (which was responsible for the expedition) looked further, to Baghdad, the fabulous medieval city of the Caliphs, some 500 miles up the Euphrates from Basra. Purely military considerations too enticed the British command to deepen their bridgehead round Basra, not least the apparent feebleness of the Turkish army. At the end of August the British began the long march to Baghdad, with shade temperatures exceeding 120° Fahrenheit. Such an advance along a river winding through a desert demanded copious river transport and a well-organized base and supply port at Basra. The government of India and the Indian army, used to punitive expeditions against the Pathan, had provided neither. To all the usual drawbacks of hasty improvisation the Indian authorities added their own brand of incompetence and muddle. Despite a supply bottleneck at Basra and a desperate shortage of river craft, the field force commander, Charles Townshend, a bold general who modelled himself on the young Bonaparte, pushed rapidly on, gambling on reaching Baghdad before his precarious lines of communication starved him to a halt. On 22 November 1915 he attacked the Turks entrenched in a strong position at Ctesiphon, some 20 miles from Baghdad. Townshend's plan was to hold the Turks with a frontal attack while he hooked around their left flank. Unfortunately his available force was not large enough to carry out such a plan. Turkish artillery and machine guns took a fearful toll of British and Indian troops advancing across ground as flat and devoid of cover as a table; Townshend's attacking infantry division lost more than half its effectives killed and wounded. Under the shadow of the great ruined Arch of Ctesiphon, all that remained of the ancient city of that name, Townshend's hope of reaching Baghdad finally died. He fell back into the mud-built Arab town of Kut al-Amarah, where his superiors instructed him to stand fast pending the arrival of fresh forces. Soon he and his army were cut off and under siege.

Now began the real time of horror for the British and Indian soldiers in Mesopotamia. The continued supply bottleneck at the port of Basra and the lack of river craft (Thames pleasure steamers were sent all the way to the Persian Gulf under their own steam as part of the desperate efforts at remedy) placed tight limits on the size of the relief force. Its commander, Lieutenant-General Sir Fenton Aylmer, strove again and again to break through the Turkish defences and rescue Townshend in Kut. The British losses were equal in proportion to the number of troops engaged to the losses in any battle on the Western Front. In Mesopotamia there existed no well-organized and thoroughly equipped medical service as in France, but a Crimean-style shambles, thanks to the incompetence of the government of India and the Indian army medical administration. Men lay with untreated, gangrenous wounds amid their own excreta on the decks of vessels making their slow way down to the primitive base hospital at Basra. One eye-witness describes the arrival of one of these craft:

When the *Mejidieh* was about three hundred yards off, it looked as if she were festooned with ropes. The stench when she was close was quite definite, and I found that what I mistook for ropes were dried stalactites of human faeces. The patients were so crowded and huddled together on the ship that they could not perform the offices of nature clear of the ship's edge.

On 29 April 1916 the 13,000-strong garrison of Kut al-Amarah, out of food and out of hope, surrendered – a disaster to British arms that made the same kind of impact on British and world opinion as the fall of Tobruk in the Second World War.

Now, at long last, muddle and hasty improvisation gave way to thorough, businesslike organization. Responsibility for Mesopotamia was transferred from the government of India to the British War Office. A first-class fighting soldier and military organizer, General Sir Stanley Maude, became Army Commander. Civilian experts and abundant resources turned Basra into an efficient supply port. The transport system and the medical services were reorganized and vastly expanded. The army in Mesopotamia grew to a ration strength of 150,000, the field force itself to 72,000.

In December 1916 Maude, outnumbering the Turks three to one in troops and with ample artillery, began a systematic advance on Baghdad. Winter rains, transforming the Mesopotamian plain into a clinging morass, did not help his march. The paradox was seen of ferocious trench warfare in the middle of an empty desert because the need for drinking water and dependence on the

Euphrates for transportation normally prevented wide turning movements. However, Maude did succeed in outflanking the powerful Turkish position that had defied British attempts to relieve Kut by marching up the other bank of the river to threaten the enemy communications. Violently attacked in front at the same time, the Turks gave way, and by 24 February 1917 were in full retreat towards Baghdad. Kut al-Amarah fell once more into British hands. On 11 March, after vain Turkish resistance, Baghdad itself was captured – another close-packed and malodorous Mesopotamian slum.

The fall of the city of the Caliphs, the prize that had beckoned the British since 1914, did not mark the end of the campaign. For the next 18 months the Turks in the north of Mesopotamia, ably advised by German officers, were to keep in play British forces 10 times larger than their own ration strength of 50,000, together with all the enormous material resources and shipping necessary to support them.

•

WHEN THE 'Michael' offensive smashed upon the over-stretched and under-strength British army in France, no fewer than 900,000 British Empire troops were locked up in Greece, Palestine, Mesopotamia and other sideshows, even if in some cases in furtherance of British imperial interests. The comparable German investment in these sideshows consisted of two weak divisions with the Bulgarians and the Asia Korps of some 6,000 soldiers supporting the Turks against Allenby.

Yet even though they had no effect on the issue of the Great

War, the Palestine and Mesopotamian campaigns were to have far-reaching consequences on world history. Behind the scenes the politicians and diplomats were already intriguing over the postwar shape of the Middle East. In 1915, in order to encourage the Arabs to rise against their Turkish overlords, the British promised Sharif Husain of Mecca that all Turkey's Arab lands should become independent. However, Husain was to be cheated of his dream of an independent Arabia from the Mediterranean shore to the Red Sea and the Gulf. From 1916 onwards the British and French secretly evolved schemes to partition these territories between themselves into spheres of interest – schemes that eventually reached fruition in the form of League of Nations mandates, when France received the mandate for Syria, and Britain those for Palestine, Jordan and the oil-rich country of Iraq.

In November 1917, in order to enlist the support of world Jewry in the Allied cause, the British War Cabinet issued the 'Balfour Declaration', ambiguously promising the Jews 'a national home' in Palestine. From the contradictory promises made to Jew and Arab, and from the conquest of the Turkish Empire by British armies, was to spring today's conflict between Israel and its Arab neighbours.

SIXTEEN

Victory and defeat

FOR BOTH SIDES ON THE WESTERN FRONT the second week of August 1918 marked a time of reappraisal following the Allied counterstrokes on the Marne on 18 July and the Somme on 8 August. Now the initiative lay in the grip of the Allies; the question for them was how best to use it. Foch, the Allied Generalissimo, urged Haig to attack again on the Somme front on 16 August. Haig, after consulting Rawlinson, the Fourth Army commander, decided to postpone the operation, however, because the German defence on this front had consolidated again – whereupon Foch peremptorily asked Haig to carry out the attack as planned. But the British Commander-in-Chief refused to alter his decision, and on 14 August visited Foch at his HQ at Sarcus to make clear to him, in Haig's own words, that 'I was responsible to my Government and fellow citizens for the handling of the British forces'. Foch had no alternative but to yield to Haig's assertion of independence. The dispute, like others later between Foch and the American Commander-in-Chief, Pershing, illustrates Foch's lack of real executive authority. In any case, he was genuinely persuaded by Haig's argument that it would be better to strike on a fresh front further north with the British Third Army. So the pattern was set for the remainder of the campaign, with Foch, though Allied Generalissimo, falling in with the strategic ideas of the British Commander-in-Chief. But by an irony, it was Foch who would be credited by Lloyd George and by British national memory with the succession of Allied victories that followed. By a further irony, British memory, while always remembering the attrition battles of 1916–17, was to forget the British army's predominant share in the victories of 1918. In fact, from the beginning of August to the end of the war the British army was to take 188,700 prisoners and 2,840 guns as against 196,070 prisoners and 3,775 guns taken by the French, Belgians and Americans together.

While Haig and Foch were arguing, Kaiser Wilhelm II was presiding over a grim and glum examination of Germany's plight at GHQ in Spa – an examination that ended in a decision to open up peace negotiations via Queen Wilhelmina of the Netherlands. Typical of the incoherence of German top leadership, no peace formula was hammered out, and no timing agreed on. No diplomatic action followed therefore; the Germans drifted in the vague hope that some future improvement in the military situation would provide a suitable springboard. A visit to GHQ on 14 August by the Emperor Karl of Austria-Hungary and his Chief of Staff likewise yielded no agreement on policy, but instead a warning that the Austrian army could not survive another winter. It would be the Allied armies, striking relentlessly home, that would decide Germany's policy for her. While the German leadership faced the fact of defeat completely bankrupt of ideas, the German soldier fought on, the skill and steadfastness of certain units such as machine-gunners and field artillery redeeming the general steady slide into moral and physical collapse.

On 21 August Haig launched his offensive with the Third Army north of the Somme between Arras and Albert, winning a limited success – limited because of the caution and rigidity of the Third Army's plan. Disappointed, Haig signalled his army commanders:

> Risks which a month ago would have been criminal to incur, ought now to be incurred as a duty. It is no longer necessary to advance in regular lines and step by step. On the contrary, each division should be given a distant objective which must be reached independently of its neighbours.

On 23 August the Third Army took Albert and the Fourth Army joined the offensive, widening the front of attack to 35 miles. In blazing August heat, the British swept over the old Somme battlefield in the course of a single weekend. On 26 August Haig launched his First Army to the attack on the River Scarpe. The German line staggered under this succession of onslaughts: on 29 August Bapaume, on the Somme front, fell to the superb New Zealand Division; on the 31st the Australian Corps took the powerful German bastion of Mont-Saint-Quentin near Péronne. The French Third Army took Noyon. In the words of the Bavarian official history, 'the German Front ached and groaned in every joint under the increasing blows... The German divisions just melted away. Reinforcements, in spite of demands and entreaties, were not forthcoming... In the circumstances, the troops deteriorated both spiritually and physically. For the most part they were burnt-out cinders.'

On 12 September it was the Americans' turn. The United States First Army, under Pershing's personal command, carried out the first all-American offensive of the war, successfully pinching out the Saint-Mihiel Salient to the east of Verdun, and taking 15,000 prisoners and 460 guns at a cost of 7,000 casualties. The President sent his congratulations: 'The boys have done what we expected of them and done it in a way we most admire. We are deeply proud of them and their Chief.'

Six days later Haig attacked again with the Fourth Army and part of the Third, with the formidable Australians again in the van. The shape of Allied strategy was becoming clear: instead of a single massive offensive, like the German 'Michael' operation, which could not be kept moving by the transport technology of the time, the Allies were launching carefully phased limited offensives up and down the front. They firmly retained the initiative by preventing the enemy from concentrating his available reserves.

On 23 September a conference of Allied commanders-in-chief at Foch's headquarters ratified ideas put forward by Haig for the next phase of the offensive: first a Franco-American attack northwards on Mézières from the Argonne Forest, followed a day later by a British attack eastwards on Cambrai and another, the day after, by the Flanders Group of Armies (including the Belgians) between the Lys and the North Sea.

Thanks to superb staff work, largely directed by Colonel George C. Marshall of the First US Army Operations Section, the bulk of the US First Army was redeployed from Saint-Mihiel to the Argonne sector alongside the French Fourth Army in time for the planned attack to be launched on 26 September. For four days the attackers struggled forward in a tangled wilderness of trees and undergrowth against a German defence in depth by machine-gunners and field artillery, finally taking the commanding height of Montfaucon and 18,000 prisoners. Yet the performance of the young American army, like that of the British 'New Army' at its debut in 1915–16, had proved brave but clumsy. In General Pershing's own words, 'It was one thing to fight a battle with well trained, well organized and experienced troops, but quite another matter to take relatively green troops and organize, train and fight them at the same time.'

The British army was now up to the formidable defences of the Hindenburg Line, some 10 miles deep, with a maze of dense belts of barbed wire. On 27 September, under cover of a dawn hurricane bombardment and supported by 16 tanks (all that were available), the First Army's Canadian Corps attacked the Canal du Nord sector, where the canal itself, now dry, constituted a special obstacle. After two days the Canadians had gained a lodgement 12 miles wide and six deep in the German defences. Meanwhile, on 28 September, the French, Belgians and British of the Flanders Group struck their blow, advancing astride the city of Ypres in a single day further than the British had advanced in four months during the Third Battle of Ypres in 1917. Next day the British Fourth Army, with the French First Army on its right, attacked the Hindenburg Line along its strongest sector on the Saint-Quentin Canal, a broad obstacle sunk between high embankments. General John Monash's plan was for the Australian Corps, with two American divisions under command, to cross the three-and-a-half-mile-wide land bridge where the Canal ran underground in a tunnel. Unfortunately, the advance of the inexperienced American troops broke down in utter confusion, wrecking Monash's carefully laid scheme. Instead it was the British 46th Division, Territorials from the English Midlands, who saved the day by crossing the Saint-Quentin Canal with lifebelts, improvised rafts and collapsible boats, and advancing more than three miles into the enemy defence system. By October Haig's armies – troops from Australia, New Zealand, Canada and the United Kingdom – had each smashed gaps right through the Hindenburg Line, leaving only sections and bastions in German hands, like the remnants of a sea wall after a great storm.

It was not only on the Western Front that September proved a month of cumulative disaster for Germany. On the 15th the Allied armies in Greece, now commanded by one of France's most thrustful generals, Louis Franchet d'Esperey, launched a general offensive against the Bulgarians. On the 29th the Bulgarians, utterly defeated and in headlong retreat, signed an armistice, the first of Germany's satellites to drop out of the war. Meanwhile, on the 19th, Allenby had struck in Palestine against the heavily outnumbered Turks. Attacks by Arab guerrillas against Turkish rail communications convinced the enemy commander, the German Liman von Sanders (the one-time defender of Gallipoli), that the British offensive would fall on his inland flank in the Judaean hills. Instead Allenby smashed open his coastal flank and dispatched massed cavalry sweeping north and east through the Plain of Esdraelon across his rear. In the Battle of Megiddo the trapped Turkish army west of the Jordan was destroyed; Turkish troops east of that river fell haplessly back towards Damascus.

The news from Bulgaria and Turkey, coming just as the Western Front seemed to be tottering on the brink of collapse, hit the German leadership hard. On 29 September another frenzied round of high-level discussions began, in which Ludendorff insisted that Germany must now have an immediate armistice. German statesmen warned that only the prompt introduction of a parliamentary constitution could stave off popular unrest, or even a revolution, at home. Thus it was that parliamentary democracy at last came to Germany – as the gift of Allied guns. A prominent liberal statesman, Prince Max of Baden, was appointed Imperial Chancellor, with an overriding task of obtaining an armistice from the Allies.

Under the impact of Haig's successes against the Hindenburg Line, the German panic grew. On 2 October an emissary from Hindenburg and Ludendorff told the Reichstag in Berlin: '...each new day brings the enemy nearer his goal, and makes him less ready to conclude a reasonable peace with us. We must accordingly lose no time. Every 24 hours that pass may make our position worse.' At these words, utter consternation seized the Reichstag members, from whom the truth about Germany's plight had been concealed up till now by the high command. On 4 October Prince Max sent a message to the United States president, Woodrow Wilson, asking for an armistice on the basis of the so-called Fourteen Points – a cloudy peace programme enunciated by Wilson in January 1918.

The German request for an armistice caught the Allies totally unprepared. Despite the Allied victories since 18 July, few Allied leaders except Haig himself thought that Germany was close to final defeat. For example, Winston Churchill, now Minister of Munitions, and Sir Henry Wilson, Chief of the Imperial General Staff, were busy planning for the 1919 campaign. Now, like outwardly solid timber mined away within by years of rot, German power suddenly crumbled before Allied eyes.

The Great War had sprung the last of all its surprises on the combatants: the abrupt prospect of its end.

No joint Allied war aims – and hence peace terms – had ever been drawn up; instead each nation had evolved its own objectives during the long struggle. France wanted back her lost provinces of Alsace and Lorraine and the evacuation of her occupied territory. Conscious of her weakness of population and resources in comparison to Germany, she wanted security too, and she looked to German disarmament and Allied military occupation of the Rhineland to accomplish this. More, she dreamed of undoing the unification of Germany by promoting the independence of German states, such as Bavaria. Britain, for her part, was determined that the German challenge to British naval supremacy should be eliminated for ever. She also had her eye on various portions of the German and Turkish empires in Africa and the

Middle East. Just as France meant Germany to pay in reparations for all the immense damage done on her national territory, the British intended that the Germans should make reparation for Britain's colossal loss of merchant shipping at the hands of the U-boat. Italy hoped for choice territorial pickings at the expense of Austria and Turkey.

Since 1915 another kind of war aim had emerged among liberals in English-speaking countries – an idealistic vision of a new world order based on the rule of law and guaranteed by a League of Nations. Disarmament would succeed the pre-war arms race; reconciliation and peaceful brotherhood between peoples would replace the Darwinian struggle between nation states, for some of the progressives who had opposed war in 1914 had by 1918 embraced it as a righteous crusade against autocratic and militaristic tyranny; to them it had become, in Woodrow Wilson's phrase, a war to make the world safe for democracy. This vision of a new world order had been passionately taken up by Woodrow Wilson himself, for the moment the most powerful among statesmen. It found its most influential pronouncement in his Fourteen Points, which called for the evacuation of occupied territories in Belgium, France, Russia, Romania and Serbia, and the return of Alsace-Lorraine to France. It called for the development of self-government for the peoples of Austria-Hungary and the Turkish Empire. It proclaimed that an independent Polish state should be created. It asked for the removal of barriers to international trade; for absolute freedom of navigation upon the seas in peace and war (which would, if accepted, prevent Britain in a future conflict stopping neutral vessels carrying contraband goods to enemy ports, as under her current system of blockade). Wilson demanded 'open covenants of peace openly arrived at' in place of traditional secret diplomacy, together with a 'general association of nations' to protect the independence and territorial integrity of great and small nations alike. Yet the language of the Fourteen Points was imprecise, lending itself to different interpretations and dangerous misunderstandings.

Now, in October 1918, under hounding pressure of time, the Allies had to hammer out specific agreed terms to offer an enemy who had asked for an armistice based on the Fourteen Points. What did the Fourteen Points really mean? The confusions within Germany's leadership were mirrored by parallel confusions and arguments within Allied councils. The Allied confusions were the worse because Woodrow Wilson more than once replied to German notes without consulting his Allies first – a sign equally of his own arrogance and of the passing of power from an exhausted Europe to a buoyant America. The Germans, counting on the idealism of the Fourteen Points, expected relative leniency; the Allies, however, screwed their specific terms tighter with every lurch forward made by their armies in the field, every fresh realization of Germany's weakness.

It did nothing to soften Allied hearts that on 4 and 10 October U-boats sank two passenger ships with heavy loss of life, and thereafter it was only the British government and its Commander-in-Chief in the field who still counselled moderation lest Germany should be driven by despair to fight on through the winter. Haig further feared that too harsh an eventual peace might spur Germany to revenge.

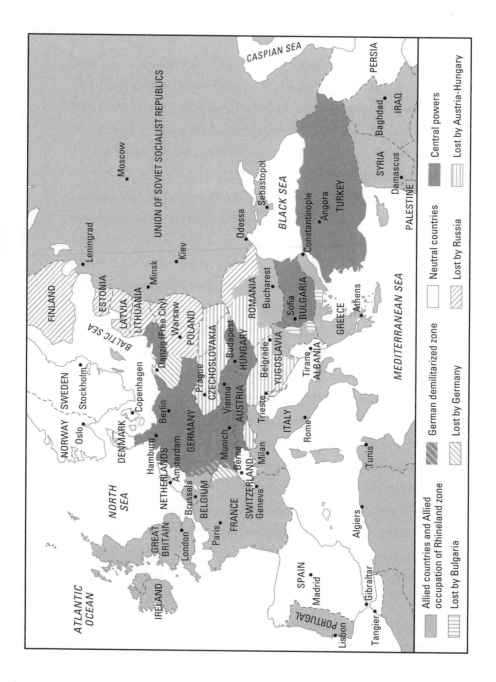

While the notes passed to and fro, the condition of the German army decayed even faster. On 18 October, the day after Haig took the great French city of Lille, a German army group commander reported to the Imperial Chancellor that 'the morale of the troops has suffered seriously and their power of resistance diminishes daily. They surrender in hordes.' A world epidemic of influenza sweeping across central Europe added to the miseries of the underfed German people; on 15 October 1,700 died from it in Berlin alone. On 25 October Ludendorff, whose erratic and ill-judged leadership had brought Germany to defeat, was dismissed. The European fortress defended so tenaciously for four years by Germany and her allies now began to crumble down on every front. Between 24 and 27 October an Allied offensive at Vittorio Veneto in Italy threw the Austrian army back in final rout. On 30 October, with Allenby's troops in Damascus and Aleppo, Turkey signed an armistice. In the first week of November Haig took Valenciennes; the French and Americans swept up to a line from Mézières to Sedan; and the Germans abandoned the Belgian coast. On 3 November Austria-Hungary too signed an armistice, and her empire, to preserve which she had sent the fatal ultimatum to Serbia in July 1914, fell apart. Czechoslovakia, Hungary and Yugoslavia proclaimed their independent nationhoods, while in Vienna the Habsburg Emperor Karl was forced to abdicate.

Opposite: **Europe after the war.** Alsace and Lorraine were given back to France, and Belgium was given more territory. An independent Poland was created from former Russian, German and Austrian territories. The new states of Finland, Estonia, Lithuania and Latvia were created from the former Tsarist Empire. The new states of Czechoslovakia and Yugoslavia were created from the former Austrian Empire.

The second of the proud imperial monarchies of 1914 had fallen, leaving behind it a huge power vacuum in the heart of Europe. That same day the German fleet at Kiel mutinied rather than make a sortie against the British. On 5 November Ludendorff's successor, General Wilhelm Gröner, reported on the state of the army in the west: 'We can hold out long enough for negotiations. If we are lucky the time might be longer; if we are unlucky, shorter.' The German home front was foundering too. In streets where once the glossy bourgeois had strolled and the Kaiser's brilliant soldiers had goose-stepped by, shabby mobs ranged about. Russian-style soviets were set up in the big cities, and in Munich a Bavarian Republic replaced the royal house of Wittelsbach.

On 8 November the German armistice delegation met Allied representatives led by Foch in a restaurant car in a siding within the Forest of Compiègne. The Germans had now acknowledged that they must accept without haggling the Allied interpretation of the Fourteen Points. They had yielded to Allied pressure, above all from Wilson, that the Kaiser's autocracy must be replaced by a democratic republic. Next day, while the armistice discussions continued at Compiègne, Spartacists (German Communists) seized the imperial palace in Berlin and proclaimed a soviet republic. Their rivals, the Social Democrats, retorted by proclaiming a socialist republic from the steps of the Reichstag. The future destiny of Germany seemed now to lie as much in question as that of Russia did in 1917, when Kerensky and Lenin had struggled for control.

Next morning the Kaiser, finally pressed into abdicating by his entourage, fled to Holland; the Hohenzollerns had followed the

Romanovs and the Habsburgs into extinction. Prince Max of Baden resigned as Chancellor in favour of the Social Democrat leader, Friedrich Ebert, a saddler's son, and later to be the first President of the German Republic. Faced with the Spartacist threat to turn Germany into a Communist state, Ebert and General Gröner swiftly made a secret deal by telephone: the army would support Ebert's new regime if Ebert in return would preserve the army as an institution under its present officer corps. This deal was to save Germany from Communism but render the new democratic Germany dependent on the army leadership. Thus it was that the confusions and humiliations of the hour of imperial Germany's defeat shaped the character and destiny of the republican Germany of the 1920s.

At five o'clock in the morning of 11 November 1918, the 1,586th day of the war, the German delegation at Compiègne signed the armistice, by which the German army was to hand over the bulk of its weapons and aircraft, the German navy was to be interned, and the Allied forces were to occupy the Rhineland and bridgeheads across the Rhine – terms which, with the Fourteen Points, foreshadowed the peace terms eventually enshrined in the Treaty of Versailles, signed on 28 June 1919. Thus the nature of the peace itself, like that of the new Germany, was determined by the way war ended – and even before it had ended.

In the morning of 11 November the last few men were being killed out of the 12 million servicemen from all the belligerent nations who fell during the conflict. At 11 a.m. the firing stopped; soldiers stood upright in unaccustomed safety listening to the birdsong, marvelling that they had survived, mourning the dead.

The Great War was over. For the moment, the Allies had achieved their supreme objective of putting an end to the menace of Germany's overweening power and ambition. It only remained for the peacemakers to render this achievement permanent.

The political and social order of the Europe of 1914 had perished in the struggle, and amid its wreckage modern Europe was being born: a Europe of the masses rather than the privileged few; of small new nation states in place of empires; a Europe weakened in power and influence, lying between a now Communist Russia and a United States newly emerged from isolation.

The victorious peoples looked to the future with elation and hope, irrationally but understandably believing that the bitterness, loss and destruction of the greatest war in history must supply a sound foundation for the building of a better world. On Armistice Night they cheered and sang and drank and kissed.

But in a German military hospital at Pasewalk near Stettin, Corporal Adolf Hitler, recovering from a British gas attack, raged in his heart over Germany's humiliation, and dreamed of the part he might play in her resurgence.

Appendix I

CHRONOLOGY OF THE GREAT WAR

1914

28 June	Archduke Franz Ferdinand of Austria-Hungary assassinated in Sarajevo by a member of the Serbian Black Hand group
23 July	Austria-Hungary demands that Serbia arrest leaders of the Black Hand group
24 July	Serbia appeals to Russia for help
25 July	Serbia refuses to hand over leaders of the Black Hand group
28 July	Austria-Hungary declares war on Serbia
1 Aug	Germany declares war on Russia
3 Aug	Germany declares war on France
4 Aug	Helmut von Moltke orders the Schlieffen Plan to proceed
	German troops enter neutral Belgium
	Great Britain declares war on Germany
	President Woodrow Wilson declares a policy of US neutrality
7 Aug	Lord Kitchener calls for 100,000 volunteers to join the British army
12 Aug	Heavy siege howitzers used against Liège Forts
	Austria-Hungary invades Serbia
14 Aug	French troops enter Lorraine
17 Aug	Russia invades East Prussia
22 Aug	British Expeditionary Force (BEF) arrives in France
23 Aug	Battle of Mons begins
	Japan declares war on Germany
24 Aug	Plan 17 abandoned by the French army
26 Aug	Battle of Tannenberg begins
28 Aug	Battle of Heligoland Bight
2 Sept	War Propaganda Bureau writers' conference
6 Sept	Battle of the Marne begins
13 Sept	German army attacked by French troops on the River Aisne
25 Sept	Battle of Albert
1 Oct	Battle of Arras
5 Oct	First German aircraft shot down by an Allied plane

15 Oct	First Battle of Ypres begins
16 Oct	Canadian troops arrive in Great Britain
29 Oct	Turkey joins the central powers
21 Nov	Anglo-Indian invasion of Mesopotamia
8 Dec	Battle of the Falkland Islands
21 Dec	First German air raid on Britain
25 Dec	Unofficial Christmas truce on the Western Front

1915

14 Jan	Swakopmund occupied by South African forces
24 Jan	Battle of Dogger Bank
10 March	BEF attacks at Neuve Chapelle
18 March	Allied naval attack on the Dardanelles
22 April	German gas attack opens the Second Battle of Ypres
25 April	Allied landings at Gallipoli
7 May	Sinking of the liner *Lusitania* off the Irish coast
9 May	Artois offensive
23 May	Italy declares war on Austria-Hungary
25 May	Germany abandons the Ypres offensive
	British PM Herbert Asquith forms a coalition government
31 May	First Zeppelin raid on London
23 June	Start of the First Isonzo offensive
6 Aug	Suvla Bay offensive at Gallipoli
5 Sept	Grand Duke Nikolai sacked as Russian Commander-in-Chief; Tsar Nicholas II takes command of the army
11 Sept	First tank demonstrated to British military leaders
25 Sept	Anglo-French offensive at Artois-Loos
5 Oct	Allied troops land at Salonika
12 Oct	Nurse Edith Cavell executed
19 Dec	Sir Douglas Haig replaces Sir John French as Commander-in-Chief of the BEF

1916

2 Feb	Great Britain introduces conscription
21 Feb	German Verdun offensive begins
9 March	Germany declares war on Portugal
31 May	Battle of Jutland
4 June	Russian Brusilov offensive
5 June	Lord Kitchener drowned at sea off the Orkney Islands
1 July	Start of the Anglo-French Somme offensive
9 Aug	Italian Gorizia offensive

28 Aug	Italy declares war on Germany
29 Aug	Paul von Hindenburg becomes German Chief of Staff
15 Sept	British tanks first used at Flers-Courcelette
24 Oct	Douaumont Fort at Verdun recaptured by the French
18 Nov	Somme offensive ends
29 Nov	David Beatty replaces Sir John Jellicoe as Commander-in-Chief of the Grand Fleet
6 Dec	David Lloyd George becomes British Prime Minister
12 Dec	Robert Nivelle replaces Joseph Joffre as Commander-in-Chief of the French army

1917

19 Jan	Zimmermann telegram intercepted by Great Britain
11 March	British capture Baghdad
15 March	Tsar Nicholas II of Russia abdicates
26 March	Battle of Gaza begins
6 April	United States declares war on Germany
9 April	Start of the Nivelle offensive
	Start of the Arras offensive
12 April	Canadian army captures Vimy Ridge
16 April	Second Battle of the Aisne begins
17 April	French tanks used for the first time in battle
15 May	Henri-Philippe Pétain replaces Robert Nivelle as Commander-in-Chief of the French army
16 May	Maria Bochkareva forms Russia's Women's Battalion
19 May	John Pershing appointed Commander-in-Chief of the American Expeditionary Force (AEF)
7 June	British attack at Messines
25 June	First United States troops arrive in France
29 June	Greece declares war on the central powers
6 July	T. E. Lawrence and the Arabs capture Aquaba
17 July	George V changes the British royal family name from Saxe-Coburg-Gotha to Windsor
31 July	Third Battle of Ypres
1 Sept	Germany takes northernmost end of the Russian Front in the Riga offensive
12 Oct	British offensive at Passchendaele
24 Oct	Italian Caporetto offensive
18 Nov	Sir Frederick Maude, commander of the Anglo-Indian forces in Mesopotamia, dies of cholera in Baghdad
20 Nov	British massed tank attack at Cambrai

| 21 Nov | Bolshevik government disbands Women's Battalion |
| 7 Dec | United States declares war on Austria-Hungary |

1918

8 Jan	US President Wilson announces the Fourteen Points peace programme
3 March	Russia concludes independent peace negotiations with Germany in the treaty of Brest-Litovsk
21 March	Start of the German spring offensive
29 March	Ferdinand Foch appointed Allied coordinator in France
27 May	Third Battle of the Aisne begins
4 July	Battle of Le Hamel
15 July	Second Battle of the Marne
16 July	Former Tsar Nicholas II of Russia and his family are murdered by the Bolsheviks
20 July	German retreat at the Marne
8 Aug	Second Battle of the Somme
21 Aug	British breakthrough at Albert
12 Sept	United States St Mihiel offensive
19 Sept	Battle of Megiddo begins the British offensive in Palestine
26 Sept	Start of the Meuse-Argonne offensive
27 Sept	British Canal du Nord offensive
3 Oct	Max von Baden appointed Chancellor of Germany
4 Oct	Germany and Austria send peace notes to US President Woodrow Wilson requesting an armistice
5 Oct	British forces breach the Hindenburg Line
23 Oct	Italian Vittorio Veneto offensive
30 Oct	Turkey concludes an armistice with the Allies
3 Nov	German fleet mutinies at Kiel
	Trieste falls to the Allies
9 Nov	Kaiser Wilhelm II of Germany abdicates
10 Nov	German republic is founded
11 Nov	Armistice day; fighting ceases at 11 a.m.
14 Dec	David Lloyd George wins the British General Election

1919

12 Jan	Paris Peace Conference begins
6 Feb	German National Assembly meets in Weimar
14 Feb	Draft covenant of the League of Nations completed
28 June	Treaty of Versailles signed
19 July	Cenotaph unveiled in London

Appendix II
CASUALTIES

Owing to incomplete statistical records in some countries, full and accurate casualty figures will never be known. The total death toll sustained by the armed services of the belligerents may be reckoned as between 10 and 13 million. The national totals of dead were as follows:

Russia 1,700,000 according to incomplete figures. (The true total is likely to have been nearly double.)

Germany 1,808,545 according to official figures. (This is probably an understatement.)

France 1,385,300 (including 58,000 colonials) dead and missing.

United Kingdom 744,702

British Empire (excluding United Kingdom) 202,321

Austria-Hungary 1,200,000 according to conjectural figures.

Italy 460,000

Turkey 325,000 according to highly incomplete figures.

United States 115,660 (including those who died of disease in the USA).

These figures are taken from *Statistics of the Military Effort of the British Empire during the Great War*, HMSO, London, 1922.

Further reading

Barker, Arthur J., *The Neglected War: Mesopotamia 1914–1919*, Faber, London, 1967.
Barnett, Correlli, *The Swordbearers: Studies in Supreme Command in the First World War*, Eyre & Spottiswoode, London, 1963.
—— *Britain and Her Army 1509–1970*, Allen Lane, London, 1970.
Beckett, Ian F. W. and Simpson, Keith (eds), *The Nation in Arms*, Manchester University Press, Manchester, 1985.
Blake, Robert (ed), *The Private Papers of Douglas Haig, 1914–1919*, Eyre & Spottiswoode, London, 1952.
Bond, Brian (ed), *The First World War and British Military History*, Clarendon Press, Oxford, 1991.
Bond, Brian and Cave, Nigel (eds), *Haig: A Reappraisal Seventy Years On*, Leo Cooper, London, 1999.
Bourne, J. M., *Britain and the Great War 1914–1918*, Edward Arnold, London, 1989.
Cecil, Hugh and Liddle, Peter (eds), *Facing Armageddon*, Leo Cooper, London, 1996.
Corns, Cathryn and Hughes-Wilson, John, *Blindfold and Alone: British Military Executions in the Great War*, Cassell, London, 2001.
Dennis, Peter and Grey, Jeffrey (eds), *1918: Defining Victory* (Proceedings of the Chief of Army's History Conference held at the National Convention Center, Canberra, 29 September 1998), Army History Unit, Dept of Defence, Canberra, 1999.
Farrar-Hockley, Anthony, *Death of an Army*, Arthur Barker, London, 1967.
—— *The Somme*, Batsford, London, 1966.
Ferguson, Niall, *The Pity of War*, Allen Lane, London, 1998.
Fischer, Fritz, *Germany's Aims in the First World War*, Chatto & Windus, London, 1967.
French, David, *The Strategy of the Lloyd George Coalition*, Clarendon Press, Oxford, 1995.
Fussell, Paul, *The Great War and Modern Memory*, Oxford University Press, London, 1975.
Gilbert, Martin, *The First World War*, Weidenfeld & Nicolson, London, 1994.
Griffith, Paddy, *Battle Tactics of the Western Front*, Yale University Press, Newhaven, 1994.
Griffith, Paddy (ed), *British Fighting Methods in the Great War*, Frank Cass, London, 1996.
Grigg, John, *Lloyd George: War Leader 1916–1918*, Allen Lane, London, 2002.
Harris, J. P. with Barr, Niall, *Amiens to the Armistice: The B.E.F. in the Hundred Days' Campaign: 8 August – 11 November 1918*, Brasseys, London, 1998.
Holmes, Richard, *The Western Front*, BBC Books, London, 1999.
Horne, Alistair, *The Price of Glory: Verdun, 1916*, Macmillan, London, 1962; New York, St Martin's Press, 1962. (abridged edition: Penguin, Harmondsworth, 1964).
Howard, Michael, *The First World War*, Oxford University Press, Oxford, 2002.
Hughes, Matthew and Seligman, Matthew (eds), *Leadership in Conflict 1914–1918*, Leo Cooper, London, 2000.
Keegan, John, *The First World War*, Hutchinson, London, 1998.

Klein, Holger (ed), *The First World War in Fiction*, Macmillan, London, 1976.

Marwick, Arthur, *The Deluge: British Society and the First World War*, Macmillan, London, 1973.

—— *Women at War 1914–1918*, Fontana in association with The Imperial War Museum, London, 1977.

Neillands, Robin, *The Great War Generals on the Western Front 1914–18*, Robinson, London, 1998.

Palmer, Alan, *The Gardeners of Salonika*, André Deutsch, London, 1965.

Pares, Sir Bernard, *The Fall of the Russian Monarchy: A Study of Evidence*, Jonathan Cape, London, 1939; Knopf, New York, 1939.

Passingham, Ian, *Pillars of Fire: The Battle of Messines Ridge, June 1917*, Sutton Publishing, Stroud, 1998.

Prior, Robin and Wilson, Trevor, *Command on the Western Front: The Military Career of Sir Henry Rawlinson*, Blackwell, Oxford, 1992.

Rhodes James, Robert, *Gallipoli*, Papermac, London, 1989.

Sheffield, Gary, *Leadership in the Trenches*, Macmillan in association with King's College London, Basingstoke, 2000.

Simkins, Peter, *Kitchener's Army: The Raising of the New Armies, 1914–16*, Manchester University Press, Manchester, 1988.

—— *Chronicles of the Great War: The Western Front 1914–1918*, Bramley Books, Godalming, 1997.

Spears, Edward, *Liaison 1914: A Narrative of the Great Retreat*, Eyre & Spottiswoode, London, 1968.

Steele, Nigel and Hart, Peter, *Passchendaele: The Sacrificial Ground*, Cassell, London, 2000.

Steiner, Zara S. *Britain and the Origins of the First World War*, Macmillan, London, 1977.

Stevenson, David, *The First World War and International Politics*, Oxford University Press, Oxford, 1988.

Stone, Norman, *The Eastern Front 1914–1917*, Hodder & Stoughton, London, 1975.

Strachan, Hew, *The First World War, Volume I: To Arms*, Oxford University Press, Oxford, 2001.

Terraine, John, *Haig: The Educated Soldier*, Hutchinson, London, 1963.

—— *Mons: The Retreat to Victory*, Batsford, London, 1960.

—— *The Road to Passchendaele: The Flanders Offensive of 1917 – A Study in Inevitability*, Leo Cooper, London, 1977.

—— *The Smoke and the Fire: Myths and Anti-Myths of War 1861–1945*, Sidgwick & Jackson, London, 1980.

—— *To Win a War*, Sidgwick & Jackson, London, 1978.

—— *White Heat: The New Warfare 1914–18*, Sidgwick & Jackson, London, 1982.

Terraine, John (ed), *General Jack's Diary 1914–18*, Eyre & Spottiswoode, London, 1964.

Travers, Tim, *How the War was Won*, Routledge, London, 1992.

Williams, John, *The Home Fronts: Britain, France and Germany 1914–1918*, Constable, London, 1972.

Wilson, Trevor, *The Myriad Faces of War*, Polity Press, Cambridge, 1986.

Winter, Jay, *The Great War and the British People*, Macmillan, London, 1985.

Index

PICTURE CREDITS

Section one
Hulton Getty; Hulton Getty; Popperfoto; Hulton Getty; Imperial War Museum;
Imperial War Museum; Hulton Getty; Imperial War Museum; Imperial War Museum;
Imperial War Museum; René Dazy; Imperial War Museum; Imperial War Museum;
Robert Harding; Scherl/SV-Bilderdienst

Section two
Imperial War Museum; Imperial War Museum; Imperial War Museum; Robert
Harding; Imperial War Museum; Imperial War Museum; Imperial War Museum;
Novosti Photo Library; Hulton Getty; Imperial War Museum

Section three
Imperial War Museum; Popperfoto; Imperial War Museum; Novosti; Imperial War
Museum; Fiore; Hulton; Imperial War Museum; Corbis; Imperial War Museum;
Imperial War Museum

Section four
Roger-Viollet; Imperial War Museum; Imperial War Museum; Imperial War Museum;
Imperial War Museum; Hulton Getty; Imperial War Museum; Imperial War Museum;
René Dazy; René Dazy